Advance Praise for L. Experience Movement

"John Gardner is a titan within higher education, yet so willingly invites us into his living room and offers a level of uncommon personal vulnerability that is both humble yet self-aware. This book is a must-read for any aspiring practitioner in the field of student success. While John's career road map is unique to him, this book brilliantly weaves together his personal story with substantive advice and intentional reflective moments that will surely inspire readers to think differently in and out of the office."—*Nii Kpakpo Abrahams*, *Director of the First Year Experience, Butler University*

"Over my nearly 6 decades as a higher educational professional, I had the privilege of working with and learning from many of our profession's most innovative leaders—innovators who shaped our nation's colleges and universities, who introduced powerful approaches to teaching and learning, who created programs and services that enabled more students to enter college and to succeed. John Gardner, a man I've known for nearly 40 years, was one of them. And he's the only one I know who left his mark on the academy by creating a movement, a man who in 1987 was described by the *Chronicle of Higher Education* as the *self-appointed spokesperson for largest educational minority*—first-year students. *Launching the First-Year Experience Movement* is a must-read for established higher education scholars, leaders, senior administrators, policy makers, support staff who work with first-year students, and graduate students who are considering a higher education career that focuses on success."—*Louis S. Albert*, *PhD, Professor of Practice, Division of Educational Leadership and Innovation, Mary Lou Fulton Teachers College, Arizona State University*

"I have always appreciated that the *first-year experience* defied the expected 'elevator pitch' simplicity common to reform fads in higher education. This book makes clear that the intellectual depth of the international reform movement entrusted to our care is a reflection of its prime mover."—*Kurt Ewen*, *PhD, Chief of Staff and Vice Chancellor, Strategy, Planning and Institutional Effectiveness, Houston Community College*

"*Launching the First-Year Experience Movement: The Founder's Journey* is a tour de force! I was captivated, engaged, and inspired by the replicable and innovative stories that illustrated the origin and development of the student success movement. Gardner's book serves as a call to action for all of us to do more for students and for equity in the academy. I want to be John Gardner when I grow up!"—*Jody S. Fournier*, PhD, Provost, Capital University

"John N. Gardner's *Launching the First-Year Experience Movement* is a must-read for anyone interested in the field of student success. Gardner, one of higher education's leading scholars and thinkers, offers a wealth of insight and wisdom in this delightful and insightful memoir. Through his own experiences as a higher education leader and innovator, Gardner provides a unique and important case study of how to effectively make a difference in our field."—*Dan Friedman*, Director, University 101 Programs, University of South Carolina

"Few initiatives in higher education over the past 5 decades have experienced the sustained national adaptation and influence of what modestly began as the 'University 101' program launched by John Gardner and his colleagues at the University of South Carolina in 1974. Consequently, Gardner's memoir, *Launching the First-Year Experience Movement*, documents a very personal journey and also the continuing programmatic evolution and institutional impact of what emerged from a directive to help 'transform university culture' at the University of South Carolina—to 'humanize it' and to make it more 'student centered.' These were—and continue to be—ambitious goals for any college or university. Gardner's chronicle reminds us of the distance traveled over 5 decades, and also of the challenges that remain." —*Kenneth C. Green*, The Campus Computing Project

"John Gardner's timely and sobering memoir is a practical guide for professionals at any stage. The seamless transitions from chapter to chapter embody many lessons that contribute to the overall advocacy of higher education. Such defining perspectives and experiences shared from the text can serve as stimulus to encourage significant change in equity, social justice, and the overall success of collegiate students. I encourage all practitioners and scholars at any point in their higher education tenure to read."—***Michael Igbonagwam***, *EdD, Program Manager, Office of Strategic Initiatives and Engagement, South Carolina Commission on Higher Education*

"All college and university educators would benefit by understanding the origin of the First-Year Experience movement. John N. Gardner's account offers a passionate and instructive story loaded with wisdom and advice about the importance of the first year of college as a foundational experience of undergraduate education."—***Jillian Kinzie***, *Interim Codirector, National Survey of Student Engagement, Indiana University Bloomington*

"At a time in our country where we all could use some direction, John Gardner candidly shares his journey from a lost college freshman to an international leader in higher education. His tale serves as a blueprint to inspire, lead, and assist others in avoiding pitfalls on the journey to achieve their life's work. Instructive from beginning to end, this is a must-read."—***Kimberly Kolodoye***, *EdD, Program Coordinator of Student Success, Professor of Learning Framework and Developmental English, Houston Community College*

"John N. Gardner has been one of the most influential figures in American higher education for decades. His pioneering work and thought leadership on the first-year experience has benefited millions of students, easing an often challenging adjustment to college. The John N. Gardner Institute for Excellence in Undergraduate Education is an authoritative voice about innovative practices in teaching and learning, which has led to students experiencing more engaging classrooms, better mentoring, and many fewer systemic barriers to learning that often most impact first-generation college students and students of color. Beginning with his own ironic, less-than-stellar start at Marietta College, Gardner reveals much in this book about his own life experiences, character, and values that shaped a movement focused on college student success."—***Leo M. Lambert***, *President Emeritus and Professor, Elon University*

"This book captivates readers with this unusual, heartfelt, life-changing adventure of my colleague and dear friend, John Gardner who is without a doubt higher education's 'Man of La Mancha.' The story of this author's life 'crusade' for students who are underserved and inequitably treated as they pursue dreams of a better life with a college diploma is a touching tale that will stir hearts and minds with a tantalizing fascination to join in the crusade. I certainly couldn't resist."—*John Lawless*, *Entrepreneur, Investor and John N. Gardner Institute Fellow*

"John Gardner's *Launching the First-Year Experience Movement* is a compelling blueprint of how to organize and mobilize to make a difference in the life of others, particularly college students. We see how John allowed the context of the civil rights movement to influence him, and how that created the subtext for his commitment to drive meaningful change in higher education. It illuminates the question: How are we allowing the current context to influence us to lead and drive positive change for our students?"—*Nicole L. McDonald*, *PhD, Senior Vice President, Transformation Initiatives, Johnson C. Smith University*

"All of us who are committed to equity and excellence in higher education owe a debt of gratitude to John N. Gardner for his willingness to tell the story that underlies his unswerving commitment to ensuring academic success for *all* students, especially first-generation and ethnic minorities. John was an equity ally long before the current era of diversity, equity, and inclusion (DEI). As a Black baby boomer and three-time university president, I have long been inspired by how John Gardner has used his agency to be a voice for historically disenfranchised populations. This book should be on the *required* reading list for current and aspiring university leaders."—*Charlie Nelms*, *Indiana University, President-in-Residence, United Negro College Fund*

"John Gardner's book is essentially the story of twin journeys. The first of these is the personal voyage of a young man starting from a privileged white background via service in the Air Force at the time of the Vietnamese war, through a developing career as a university teacher to his present status as the central figure in the First-Year Experience Movement. The other journey is that of universities and colleges themselves coming to appreciate the vital importance of the learning (and hence teaching) experienced by students during their first year. A large part of this development is due to the initiative and work of Gardner, through his many years of consultancies, international conferences, and more recently through the work of the John N. Gardner Institute for Excellence in Undergraduate Education. The book gives a splendid insight into how ideas may be transformed into practice within the context of higher education and how a change agent can influence and expedite that transformation. It will appeal to a wide range of university and college teachers as a case study of a contemporary success story in how we care for the intellectual development of our students, especially during their vital early experiences."—*Brian E. Oldham*, *Head of Educational Development, Transatlantic Consultant, Teesside University, UK (retired)*

"Behind all successful leading-edge ideas is the vision of a genius, and this is ever so evident in John N. Gardner's authentic account of his journey in college and the military. In this one-of-a-kind memoir, he recounts epiphanous moments in his life including the people and events that inspired him to create some of higher education's most impactful innovations, chief among them what is known as 'the first-year experience.' If you are a champion of student success, I believe my friend and colleague, John, would want you to read his book to reflect on your own life journey, your own epiphanies and allow these learnings to inspire creative ideas about how to positively impact all students especially those who are first-generation, low-income, and racially minoritized—and then, take transformative action to become an equity warrior and to fashion the next generation of the American student success movement. My own hope is to honor John's legacy in this profound fashion."—*Laura I. Rendón, author of* Sentipensante Pedagogy: Educating for Wholeness, Social Justice, and Liberation, Second Edition, *Stylus*

"For decades, John Gardner has shaped the conversation on college student success, but *Launching the First-Year Experience Movement* does more than simply reflect on how to improve college outcomes. Rather, Gardner takes us on a personal journey and asks us to reflect on how we can make our own distinct and powerful contributions to an equity-focused student success agenda."—*Tracy L. Skipper, Senior Thesis Director and Academic Advisor for the Honors College, University of South Carolina*

"*Launching the First-Year Experience Movement* is a compelling and inspirational read. John Gardner's candid and engaging life story tells the tale of how a few of his early life experiences, which could have resulted in an end to his university career, instead led to a lifelong passion to support students as they transition into, through, and out of college. He tells of how he and his colleagues spawned the FYE movement that has inspired thousands of similar programs around the world. Perhaps most importantly, he tells us how we too can have an impact in our own institutions, building on what he has learned." —*Steven M. Smith, PhD, Professor of Psychology, St. Mary's University*

"Everyone who has been in higher education for a minute knows that John Gardner is the 'Grandfather' of the First-Year Experience. Those of us who have been in higher education for many decades know that the First-Year Experience has changed the landscape from focusing on teaching the material to the student for academic success to creating an environment for student learning to create a whole person for life. In addition, it created opportunities for countless students to achieve their dream of becoming a college graduate. In this manuscript, John chronicles how this change became a movement. If this alone were all he did in this work, it would be well worth the read. However, this is truly a memoir. Like many of us who find ourselves with more years behind us than in front of us, we reflect on who and what we are and how we got here. John does exactly that! He shares with us the elements of life that created him and thus this movement—those core values that made him the staunch advocate for ALL students, and the history that allows me to call him an equity warrior."—*Aaron Thompson, President, Kentucky Post-Secondary Council for Higher Education*

"This inspiring history is much more that that alone. It is an inspiring model for the rest of higher education faculty, staff, and administrators who aspire to contribute to student success. Professor Gardner was and is willing to invite the higher education community to join him in creating new and significant institutions: the First-Year Experience and Students in Transition at the University of South Carolina, and the Gardner Institute for Excellence in Undergraduate Education in Brevard, North Carolina. The gift he gave us initially, and actively gives now, is to be colleagues with him in learning from each other as well as from his continuing visions."—*John M. Whiteley*, *Professor of Social Ecology, University of California Irvine*

LAUNCHING THE FIRST-YEAR
EXPERIENCE MOVEMENT

LAUNCHING THE FIRST-YEAR EXPERIENCE MOVEMENT

The Founder's Journey

John N. Gardner

STERLING, VIRGINIA

Published by Stylus Publishing, LLC.
22883 Quicksilver Drive
Sterling, Virginia 20166-2019

Library of Congress Cataloging-in-Publication-Data

Names: Gardner, John N., author.
Title: Launching the first-year experience movement : the founder's journey /
    John N. Gardner.
Description: Sterling, Virginia : Stylus, [2023] | Includes index. | Summary: "This
    book argues that today more than ever we need new and more student success
    leaders to step forward to make the changes that students need, and it offers the
    story of one such leader in the belief that it will help others see how they can
    make their own contribution to this movement"-- Provided by publisher.
Identifiers: LCCN 2022062264 (print) | LCCN 2022062265 (ebook) |
    ISBN 9781642674934 (paperback) | ISBN 9781642674927 (cloth) |
    ISBN 9781642674941 (pdf) | ISBN 9781642674958 (epub)
Subjects: LCSH: Gardner, John N. | College teachers--United States--Biography. |
    College administrators--United States--Biography. | College student development
    programs--United States--History. | College freshman--United States.
Classification: LCC LA2317.G255 A3 2023 (print) | LCC LA2317.G255 (ebook) |
    DDC 378.1/2092 [B]--dc23/eng/20230125
LC record available at https://lccn.loc.gov/2022062264
LC ebook record available at https://lccn.loc.gov/2022062265

13-digit ISBN: 978-1-64267-492-7 (cloth)
13-digit ISBN: 978-1-64267-493-4 (paperback)
13-digit ISBN: 978-1-64267-494-1 (library networkable e-edition)
13-digit ISBN: 978-1-64267-495-8 (consumer e-edition)

Printed in the United States of America

All first editions printed on acid free paper that meets the American National
Standards Institute Z39-48 Standard.

Bulk Purchases

Quantity discounts are available for use in workshops and for staff development.

Call 1-800-232-0223

First Edition, 2023

CONTENTS

PART THREE: BECOMING WHO I AM AS AN INTERNATIONAL HIGHER EDUCATION LEADER

PROLOGUE

Reflections During the Pandemic

As many authors have experienced, the actual start of putting words into a potential manuscript is preceded by many motivations, precipitating factors, thoughts about content, and especially when and how to begin. In my case I am starting this, as in the writing sense, on the annual celebration of the birthdate of Martin Luther King, Jr., January 18, 2021, about 2 weeks short of my 77th birthday.

I am going to start this book with two detailed reflections about the connection between my life and that of King. I do so to draw lessons that I hope will be applicable to my readers who I know will be of many different stages in their own life development cycle, and to the students whose success I am assuming my readers want to increase during and after college. I aspire to inspire others and thus start with reflection on the individual who inspired me in my life's work as a White man striving for justice for all.

On August 28, 1963, I first really heard Martin Luther King. "Really" in the sense of allowing what he was saying to command my attention, imagination, and my own aspirations. Many of our students have moments just like this—I know they do, and so do you. This was truly a teachable moment, an opportunity for epiphany. During my 32-year teaching career in South Carolina I often told my students that one of my hopes for them in whatever course we were experiencing together was that they would have an epiphany. I defined this for them as the realization of an insight that was powerful enough to be the basis for them of some decision that could be life-altering and transformative if, and only if, they moved that decision to action. I would disclaim to them that the epiphany had to come from my agency. It really had to come from them and their own thought processes. But it could be inspired by something they read in this course, or discussed in class, or was said by a fellow student or me. This notion of moving from powerful insight to a plan, to execution of that plan has become the structure for the final phase of my work life, as I shall explain later.

Anyway, here I was, 19 years old, just having finished my sophomore year of college, driving my car on New Jersey's Garden State Parkway, listening to a news station on the car radio. I was on the way to start a second-shift job at a factory of the American Can Company (Canco) that made beer and soda cans. This was a summer job for me, arranged by my father who was the senior corporate executive who managed 60 or so of this company's container manufacturing plants around the country. He had pushed me into this job to provide me a character-building experience as a unionized steelworker, doing some of the most dirty, heavy, loud, and monotonous factory work in America—millions of beer cans and not a drop to drink, a real torture for a college student. I was a classic "undecided" liberal arts student who had no specific idea about vocational choice or purpose. The only thing I knew for sure was that I didn't want to make beer cans for the rest of my life.

I was driving along, and the radio station switched to live coverage of the now famous March on Washington about to be headlined by Martin Luther King. Yes, I had "heard" him before, clips anyway. But I hadn't yet read any of his thinking. And it wasn't until that afternoon that I really "heard" him. As the speech unfolded, known henceforth as the "I Have a Dream" speech, I knew this was going to really be something, so I pulled over to the side of the road and gave him my full attention.

As I let his soaring, roaring words take over my consciousness, my imagination, my sense of where this speech was taking place in the past and contemporary history of my country, and where I was in my own life journey, I knew he was speaking directly to me, for the moment anyway, and for much reflection afterward.

Like most college students, I could be moved by the combination of context, message, and persona. But I had had little experience with this kind of oratory previously. Occasionally, one of my professors at Marietta College in Marietta, Ohio, would say something, or read from something in class, that would really grab me, and I would let it sink in. I knew about myself that I was a seeker. I was hungry for something that might move me, empower me, change me, and help me move beyond my life experience so far.

The only national leader whom I had ever heard, and who had any similar kind of impact on me, was President John Kennedy in his inauguration speech of January 20, 1961. In that speech he so famously asked citizens like me to ask not what our country could do for us but what we could do for our country. And I certainly didn't have an answer to that yet (but I ultimately did and still do), but President Kennedy certainly pushed me to start thinking. The answer to that question of what I could do for my country was just waiting to be formulated and answered by creating and then pursuing a dream. Along came King pushing me to develop a notion about a dream. The dream. My dream. My dreams. That's what this book is going to be all about: the journey both to those dreams and how they are still being fulfilled for the betterment of American higher education and the success of students.

I got back on the road and drove to my factory job, not knowing what the impact of that experience would be, let alone that it was going to constitute an epiphany.

My job that summer was in Canco terminology, as a "stacker." It was truly mindless. I spent 8 hours a day, often with 4 hours of overtime, pushing it to 12 hours from midnight to 4:00 a.m., lifting cartons of either 24 or 48 cans coming down "the line" on conveyor belts at the rate of 600 cans a minute. These cans were inserted into boxes that I had to lift, pull off the conveyor belt, and either "stack" on skids for fork trucks to then remove or load inside long, hot, dirty tractor-trailer trucks to be hauled away to the nearby breweries. This is what I was going to college for? No, of course not. But I was sort of trying to follow in my father's footsteps. I ultimately came to realize he did a very smart thing getting me to do that kind of work during my college summers. As had been said before by others: "The older I get the smarter my father (or mother) has become."

In the year of the stock market crash, 1929, my father had to drop out of college to go to work to support his mother. Her husband had probably (as a child I was never told the whole story) committed suicide after his business failed. This was 6 years before Social Security was enacted, thanks to my Democrats, and so my father's mother, a new widow, had no one to support her except her son, my father. He was very lucky to get even an hourly laborer job in a factory of the American Can Company doing very menial, mindless work, similar to what I was doing, but he did it so well and so impressed his superiors that he experienced a meteoric rise in this large company. Thus, by the time that I came along needing a summer job as a college student, he was the executive running every single one of these factories in the United States

As an aside, but an important one for my understanding about my own gender, one of the many things that really stayed with me from that summer job was that I observed a cohort of women very unlike my fellow female college students, women also working "on the line." My U.S. history courses in college had taught me these were the same kind of women who helped the United States to become "the arsenal of democracy" and win World War II. I was so naïve I didn't know women worked outside the home. My wealthy mother was never employed. I learned that many of the jobs these women did could not be replicated by individual men on the third shift, midnight to 7:00 a.m., because New Jersey did not allow women to work in factories after midnight. And it took two men on the "graveyard shift" to do the job of one woman during the first and second shift. Why? Because men like me lacked the requisite manual dexterity, speed, and concentration abilities to move rapidly enough and stay focused enough to avoid errors that would slow down the production pace. Today, we see the same pattern of academic ability differences between male and female students in colleges and universities.

King came back into my life 5 years later. In between the "I Have a Dream" speech and its impact on me, I had graduated from college and finished a master's degree, was drafted and volunteered for the Air Force, and was sent to a base in South Carolina as a psychiatric social worker. In the Air Force I reported to the single most influential man in my life, after my father, namely, my African American squadron commander, who ordered me to do community service in the form of adjunct teaching for the University of South Carolina during my off-duty hours. Hence, I found myself both on active duty in the U.S. Air Force and as an adjunct faculty member on the day King was murdered in Memphis, April 4, 1968.

I had a class to teach the next day and decided I would set aside the regular content I had planned to cover and instead devote the entire class period to a eulogy, an examination of the life and significance of King's work, starting with his own college days at Morehouse College in Atlanta. My students in this particular class were all White with one exception, and all of them were products of racially segregated schools in the little textile mill town of Lancaster, South Carolina, where the University of South Carolina had opened an "extension" campus 9 years before. To prepare for class, I went to the base's library and pulled several of King's books to mark passages for a series of readings I was going to use with my students the next night, readings especially from his most recent book, *Where Do We Go From Here?* The class came off fairly well, I thought, although I could tell that some of my students were in states of disbelief, not so much that King had been murdered, but that their White professor would devote so much time and respect to trying to get them, my students, to understand why King was so significant in U.S. history.

The next week when I came back to that campus to teach the class again there was a note in my campus mailbox from the campus chief executive officer asking me to come by his office before class. I did so and received from the dean a report that after my class of the previous week a delegation of my students had come to his office to complain about me as a "n____ lover." I was stunned. I could not imagine being given a similar reprimand in the Air Force, and not only because my hospital squadron commander was a Black man. This was 4 years after the Civil Rights Act, and unlike this campus community where I was an adjunct faculty member, my base was completely integrated racially. The Air Force culture would not have tolerated such openly racist leadership as I was hearing in a higher education setting. Well, thanks to King, this was the cause of another epiphany, an important insight, which moved me to action.

When the dean delivered his homily to me on the need to accommodate to racist campus and community sentiments, I was 5 months from my "DOS" (date of separation) from my Air Force tour, and I had already applied for and been offered a full-time faculty position at this very same campus. I realized then that I could not possibly survive in an environment that was so administratively hostile to my basic values. Therefore, the next day after that conversation with the dean, I wrote him a letter resigning from the full-time position I had previously accepted. I did so without another job. But I had a dream, thanks to King, that I could teach and enlighten my southern students to help them get beyond the racial prejudice we had all learned by growing up in America.

I didn't know it then, of course, but because I had taken a walk from that job, I would get another position, at another small-town southern college campus, where a year and a half later instead of having the choice to resign, I would have that choice made for me and instead was terminated. "Why?" you ask. Because in the spirit of King I had been very involved in local civil rights activism. Because of this activism, I had come to the negative attention of the chair of the board of trustees of the college that employed me. The chair ordered the college president to terminate me, which he did. That was one of the best things that ever happened to me, thanks again to King's influence, because getting fired was the impetus for me to subsequently obtain a full-time faculty job at the University of South Carolina, the institution that ultimately gave me a career and a mission that is a basis of this book. Thank you, Martin Luther King, Jr.!

And thank you, reader, for starting with me on this journey for student success. I am going to do my best to "retain" you just as I did for my students.

John N. Gardner
Pisgah Forest, North Carolina
January 18, 2021

ACKNOWLEDGMENT

I acknowledge with gratitude my editor at Stylus Publishing, David Brightman, whose faith in me led him to sign me on for still another project with him and who encouraged me to write this book in the first place. I might not have done this without his influential and perfectly timed nudge. He is truly an editor par excellence.

INTRODUCTION

Just like our students and our colleges and universities, we all have a story. In that vein, this book is a story too, of the origins and substance of an international higher education movement that came to be known as the "first-year experience." It is simultaneously a story of a life in college, my story, one educator. But it is much more than that. It can be a story for many others who will read and apply this as appropriate. It is a story of a journey to success in college and life writ large for one student but by extension for all college students, and especially now for both those students and more experienced educators who are making a life's work out of what has become known as "student success." Thus, this story is really a "transcript," a record, but not of grades, although a few are mentioned. Instead, it is a story of major milestones in U.S. and international higher education to pay more attention to the success of postsecondary students, especially those not raised in privilege like me. It is a story about events and individuals that launched a national and international movement to enable many more college students to proceed beyond the beginning college experience and complete the credential they are seeking. It is also my personal history—how I ended up spending my whole life in college, and how college can make us wiser and more successful than when we started the journey. I welcome you, reader, to this journey and hope and trust it will give you many occasions to reflect on your own story.

I am at the ideal time in life to share these reflections and counsel. I have nothing more to prove. I'm not looking for a job or career advancement. I have 56 years of professional experience from which I am drawing. For openers this is the story of how colleges can and do introduce students to life-changing perspectives and ideas. In my case it was a matter of my being introduced during college to the question "What is justice?" and then spending my entire professional life seeking ways to bring justice to underserved college students, and, in effect, becoming an "equity warrior"—but definitely "within the system."

There is a movement in the United States called by many the student success movement. This takes over from and moves beyond its predecessor, the focus on retention. If you want to either enter or advance in this field of

1

student success, what are the things you could/should do? As of now there are no doctoral programs to prepare one specifically to do this work. And the "field" is not narrowly defined by disciplinary routes and points of entry. In fact, it is just the opposite. It is open to people who are so motivated and inclined and who have the skills, abilities, attitudes, and character to succeed at this work. The field is also very fluid, meaning there are more and more points of entry all the time.

Because the student success field disproportionately focuses on low-income, minoritized populations, it is understandable that the individual backgrounds of some college or university educators would lend themselves more naturally to this work than others, especially in terms of empathy, common experiences before and during college, motivation, commitment, and race, ethnicity, and family income. But what about the larger population of faculty and staff who are more advantaged, like yours truly—those who have the motivation, interest, commitment but are *not* themselves individuals who originally came from disadvantaged circumstances? These educators are also very much needed because of their relative sheer numbers and because of the support and imprimatur they can lend to the student success movement overall. Thus, in this book I need to lay out my own unlikely origins to become a liberal, higher education, equity warrior, Democrat, and patriot.

Specifically, I am a less likely champion for higher education equity. I need to confess my White male, privileged background as the son of very well-off, very Republican, parents. My father was a member of the senior corporate executive leadership class; my mother of inherited wealth; and I had the additional privilege of growing up in New Canaan, Fairfield County, Connecticut, the so-called "Gold Coast"—one of the wealthiest per capita ZIP codes in the United States with very well-funded (by local affluent taxpayers) and high-performing local schools.

This work then will be, in effect, an autobiographical case study, that is, a set of reflections about my experience, intended to help the reader see how a person can become extremely effective as a student success higher education professional.

Key Influences

A number of the leading, seminal thinkers whose scholarship and writing contributed to the birthing of the student success field are either no longer living, retired, or have moved on in other ways. There is a need for regeneration of new leadership, intellectually and programmatically. But some of us still left in the game need to get busy and share our lessons learned while we still can.

There is a convergence of factors operating at this time. In 2020 we experienced three concurrent events that have made much more apparent the need for an expanded student success movement:

- the global COVID-19 pandemic, which made the previously existing levels of inequality all the more apparent;
- the Black Lives Matter movement and the associated murders of Black persons by law enforcement personnel and civilians; and
- the 2020 presidential election leading to the defeat of an openly racist candidate by a new president who is much more publicly open to adopting public policies to benefit all citizens. As of this writing, it remains to be seen how much he and his party can advance the equity agenda.

If then we were to see an expansion of public policy in higher education that is more supportive of efforts to close equity attainment gaps, we are going to need more, and more competent, student success educators. How do you become one of these, whether you did or did not grow up in privileged circumstances?

As an archetypal student success higher-ed educator myself, I did not enter this profession intentionally. I was ordered into it, as I shall explain later. But my life experiences did prepare me to be very successful at this work. What are those experiences and types of knowledge, insight, and skills that equip one to do this kind of work? This book is about encouraging my next generation of successors to use their experiences to become equity warriors within the system.

Caveats

The writing of such a personal narrative as this is an inherently immodest exercise. I have done my best to make sure then that I am very candid about my failures and what I lacked, my limits on empathy, wisdom, and experience as a privileged White male trying to do this work successfully.

No one person's life can exactly be replicated by others. But there are many decisions I made intentionally and opportunities I took advantage of that can be replicated. I hope that I have not given gratuitous advice, let alone appeared to be cavalier, condescending, boasting, pretentious, or promoting of any commercial services, products, and panaceas. This will not be a marketing pitch for anything in the field of shameless commerce. To the fullest extent possible I will try to acknowledge my biases, blind spots, and shortcomings as well as my foundational strengths (just as our students possess).

Using This Book for Guided Reflection

What I want to do is to simultaneously entertain, stimulate, inform, and inspire you to be successful at something very much needed by higher education and the country, student success, but which many of us did not set out to pursue.

To do this I want to present a portrait of my professional life's evolution by tracing a historical course of development with many vignettes that lead to presenting stimuli for readers' own reflections about advancing their careers and their simultaneous work on student success; generalizable lessons learned (versus what could be construed as being unique to me and not replicable); principles for excellence in student success work; and my core beliefs and principles for life success, professional and personal fulfillment, and gratification in higher education service to others.

I recognize the challenge that readers will be at different points in their professional life journeys. I will also be trying to reach early, mid, even senior career-level higher educators to try to influence their thinking and practice of student success initiatives.

I want to raise some specific questions to pose to readers to guide their reflections and decisions. I hope readers will find this book useful for their institutions. For example, I hope that this book could be used in retreat formats as a template for thinking through the design of certain student success interventions, especially those that take place in the first-year experience. A predecessor book to this one that I coauthored and is published by Stylus is even being used in a "book study club" by the entire Minnesota State public higher education system: *The Transfer Experience: A Handbook for Creating a More Equitable and Successful Postsecondary System*.

Potential audiences include these:

- college and university faculty who are considering becoming academic or student success administrators and leaders
- current academic administrators who are already engaging in or considering becoming engaged in what we now refer to as student success work
- senior higher education leaders who wish to gain more understanding about strategies for launching, sustaining, and institutionalizing innovations to increase student success
- any educator, policymaker, or philanthropy officer interested in learning about the history and impact of the first-year experience international movement to improve student success

To further this objective of creating a work for guided reflection, I have created an online compendium to accompany this book. One of the hopes that I have for this book is that it may be used in some graduate courses for students working on master's and doctoral degrees in the study of higher education. Hence, I have provided some content options that could be assignments for students. It is possible that some readers may be undergraduate or graduate student peer leaders who are preparing to coteach first-year seminars/college success courses. My reflections may help give them insights into the important roles they will be playing as successful college students influencing entering college students. And finally, I would hope that this book could even be read by undergraduates in college success courses, and that in reading and thinking about my experiences as an undergraduate they could make better choices, especially early in the college experience, to prevent what was my own near disastrous first-year experience.

Is There Anything in My Professional Life That Can Be Applied and Replicated?

I am intentionally trying to recount here the history of a higher education reform movement that is also my history, many of the components of which I maintain are replicable. Today more than ever we need new and more student success leaders to step forward from both privileged and unprivileged backgrounds. It is reasonable to ask, "What are this guy's bona fides, and why should I take seriously anything he is going to have to say to me?"

First of all, I am a proud "veteran" of both the U.S. Armed Forces and of U.S. higher education who developed and successfully pursued a *mission*. I will talk about mission in this book but not in a messianic way to proselytize. If we are to achieve at the highest levels, we have to have a mission!

We must build our lives and careers on both our successes and failures, our strengths and weaknesses. Unlike many successful people, in some ways my career has been greatly influenced by my failures. I failed initially in college and in my first professional job post military service—in the latter case failed because I was "nonrenewed" (fired) because of my civil rights activities. In truth I have based my entire professional career on the empathy and understandings I derived from nearly flunking out of college and from a penalty I paid for my early, personal, social justice crusade.

In my faculty career, I rose from the lowest instructional rank in the academy—part-time adjunct instructor—to the highest—distinguished professor. I was tenured as associate professor at age 32 and promoted to full professor at 36. And I have had my whole life since then to decide what I am going to do "when I grow up." At a very young age and at junior faculty rank, I received the highest award for teaching excellence my university employer of 32 years can confer upon any of its faculty: the Outstanding Teaching Award.

My academic career was one marked by yielding multiple times to the siren call of institutional leadership. For example, I was a faculty senator for 9 years and secretary of the (university) faculty for 3. I am the founding executive director of the widely and internationally replicated "University 101" course now found across thousands of institutions to teach students how to be successful in college. I served as vice chancellor for Academic Affairs for the five Regional Campuses of the University of South Carolina from 1983–1996, which gave me experience as a chief academic officer, understanding, and insight into the 2-year, relatively open admissions, nonresidential sector of higher education. It is in this same sector where I did my first college teaching and became so inspired to make higher education my life's work.

When I look at the ways I have been publicly affirmed as a student success leader I am reminded that I have received the highest accolades a non–student affairs professional can win, both from those on my campus and from that profession at large. Specifically, I have received the highest honors that the professional associations for the improvement of orientation, academic advising, and developmental education can bestow. And the academic community has honored me with 12 honorary degrees recognizing my work as a student success advocate. As a White higher-ed educator I was especially proud when I won special commendation from the Black faculty/staff association at my university "for outstanding service in pursuit of affirmative action."

Thankfully, the impact I have been able to have has resulted in part from recognitions that have given me imprimatur. I have been named in three different national studies as one of the "top 10" most noteworthy innovators of U.S. undergraduate education. I have been recognized as one of the 100 nationally most recognized college faculty for institutional service. I am the founder of an international higher education reform movement known as The First-Year Experience, which I will focus on in-depth in this book. My name is synonymous as the designated leading thinker for improving first-year college students' success.

In like manner I am the creator of another transition focus known as "the senior year experience." I am the coauthor of eight books about college student transitions, which have established me as a public intellectual in my own right. And I am the coauthor (with Betsy O. Barefoot) of a 35-year-old series of textbooks for first-year seminar courses. I am the founder and cofounder, respectively, of two national/international centers/institutes focused on improving undergraduate student success. This includes most notably my creation of the now 42-year-old annual Conference on The First-Year Experience. And beyond my service to the University of South Carolina, I am the cofounder with my wife, Betsy Barefoot, of a 24-year-old nonprofit organization that has served more than 500 colleges and universities and has received more than $20 million in investments from philanthropies from 1999 to 2022.

In my broader work of service, I have served my alma mater as a member of its board of trustees for 12 years; and on boards for nonprofit organizations for fellow higher education professionals, for educating gifted young musicians, for providing U.S. college students with international study and service opportunities, and a public radio station. The overarching focus of my professional life has been my commitment to be an active participant in the unfinished civil rights movement. All my work has been characterized by an overriding focus on student success and institutional loyalty—unapologetically so.

Most importantly for readers of this book, I have discovered on this journey what higher education faculty, staff, and administrators need to do to become successful at enhancing student success and more equitable outcomes.

In the online compendium that accompanies this book, there are prompts for guided reflection as well as questions and topics for discussion. The compendium also includes additional details of my professional and personal journey, especially my precollege formal education history that I experienced in both the United States and Canada. I share my experience in the belief that those of us who aspire to help undergraduate students be more successful need to know and understand the plethora of precollege educational experiences that affect their potential for success in college. The compendium can be found by scanning the following QR code or on the Stylus website at

https://styluspub.presswarehouse.com/browse/book/9781642674934/
Launching-the-First-Year-Experience-Movement#additional

PART ONE

MY COLLEGIATE JOURNEY

I

THE ALL-IMPORTANT
FIRST YEAR OF COLLEGE

The furthest thing from my thoughts as I headed off to college in the fall of 1961 was that I would ever be the founder of an international movement to improve what I eventually coined as "the first-year experience." But then that's what the first year is all about: laying the foundation for one's unanticipated success in college and adult life.

Going Off to College

I was 17-and-a-half-years-old—a totally "undecided" student whose only motivation was to get my father off my back so I could do what I really wanted to do after 1 year of college, expand my landscape service business back home. It was a long car ride from Connecticut out to Marietta, Ohio, just my father and myself. I believe we made it in 1 day and decamped at a hotel he loved from his previous visit with me there, the Hotel Lafayette, nestled in a beautiful spot at the confluence of two rivers, the Ohio and the Muskingum. That view will forever be emblazoned in my consciousness. And instead of having me check in that evening at my "dorm," he let me stay my last night in a much more upscale setting, his hotel.

The next day he gave me three pieces of advice and made two requests of me:

- Don't smoke funny looking cigarettes, by which he obviously meant marijuana (in contrast, he was a three pack–a-day smoker of conventional, unfiltered, cigarettes, which ultimately killed him).

- Don't gamble your allowance away in card games. (My allowance was $50 a month in 1961 dollars, which according to a historical currency calculator, is equivalent to $436 today.)
- Use condoms!

I acted consistently with all three of those pieces of advice. The requests:

- Go out for the crew team.
- Join a fraternity.

My actions:

- I rowed crew for my first 2 years. It was a profound character-building experience.
- I did *not* join a fraternity when I was an undergraduate but did in the 1980s as faculty advisor to a social fraternity at the University of South Carolina (USC) and served in that capacity for 16 years, even allowing the brothers to initiate me.

Homesickness: There's No Vaccine to Prevent This

Off drove my father and I was homesick already, especially for my girlfriend who was a college student in New York City. I might as well confess here to my chronic homesickness and get that out of the way. I was nearly paralyzed by it. It was a classic example of unwanted obsessive thought patterns. I just couldn't stop thinking about home—literally my father's "place," which I loved to maintain, the beauty of New England, my overall life there excluding my life as a child of an alcoholic. And my guidance counselor was right. Marietta was a beautiful small town on the banks of two rivers with the Appalachian Mountains surrounding the city. It looked like New England. Streets were paved with brick. There were lots of historical sites including my favorite, "the Mound Cemetery," about a block from the campus, an Indigenous people's burial mound site surrounded by the graves of the Revolutionary War settlers, who had created the first permanent settlement in the U.S. Northwest Territory from 1788 on.

Marietta was a quiet, peaceful town seemingly removed from everywhere but Appalachia. In terms of lifestyle and per-capita income, it was a different world from my hometown. I took long walks every day. I wrote hundreds of letters to friends, relatives, and immediate family members, and daily ones to my girlfriend. The high point of the day was retrieving whatever was in my campus mailbox. Phone calls back home were discouraged because of cost, and my parents' social class expectation was that their child had "left home" and shouldn't be heard from with any frequency. Most of all, I missed the young woman in my life. I know now that I was clinically depressed. My sense of loss was overwhelming. I had lost my former life and had not yet replaced it with anything of meaning. I had not yet developed any meaningful relationships with either peers or faculty (thankfully this would change) and certainly not with my academic advisor who at midterm told me: "Mr. Gardner, you are the stupidest kid I have ever advised!" And the college had nothing like a counseling center or even one counseling professional. I was on my own. Welcome to the world of collegiate sink or swim.

It was more than 30 years later that we conducted, at USC, research measuring homesickness among our undergraduate, residential population. Two findings stood out for me as instructive about my own experience with homesickness: (a) Male students experienced homesickness at greater levels of disruption than female students, and (b) male students went home (i.e., a proxy marker for homesickness) more frequently than female students. The take-aways were multiple. One is that in college often the behaviors students adopt to address their problems and challenges only make those circumstances worse (e.g., the more often you go home, the more homesick you become; drinking to reduce stress has negative consequences that only serve to exacerbate stress; females are better able to hunker down and develop new relationships in new settings as opposed to trying to find more "things to do," which is a more characteristic response of men).

Memories of Orientation or How Not to Orient Students for Success in College and Life

Of course, there was "orientation." This was combined with a first week of activities and rules that applied to "freshmen," one of which was we were to wear our freshman "beanie" at all times. How I hated that symbol, and later that week I burned it. I would give anything now to still have that beanie. I could put it on eBay and command a decent price, I'm sure. We could be stopped at any time anywhere on campus by any upper-class student and asked a question. If we did not answer the question to the interrogator's satisfaction, we received a summons to Kangaroo Court where sentences involving some form of ostensibly harmless indignity were meted out by the upper-class students. I did get a summons but did not appear. Today, of course, we would describe such practices as "hazing." And today, many of these practices have been driven underground and exist only informally, unsanctioned by official institutional culture. But, in contrast, hazing was official policy and practice in the vast majority of undergraduate institutions in the early 1960s, including mine. And in some ways, like today, it was just thought of as "tradition" and/or "the way we have always done things." I will remember to my grave my orientation leader. He was a senior. He was tall, handsome, so collegiate looking, calm, assured, and I told myself I would never look like this guy.

The Orientation That Really Mattered: Greek Rush

During the first week "rush" also took place, which for me was the occasion of my first values-based decision in college. One evening I was introduced to what had been a long-standing tradition of a particular fraternity, offering freshman men an all-expenses paid trip from Marietta, Ohio, up the Ohio River to Wheeling, West Virginia, about 70 miles north. What was the big deal about Wheeling? Well, this was in the era of wide-open gambling and prostitution in a number of the Ohio River Valley small cities, including Wheeling. The real point of the trip to Wheeling was to take the uninitiated men to a brothel for what it was assumed would be their first experience of a sexual act of their choice, all expenses for such being covered by their future "brothers."

When these two fraternity brothers came to my room to offer me this life-changing experience, I was flabbergasted at just the thought of it. And I did consider it, but not for long. Yes, I was looking forward to experiencing sexual intercourse for the first time. But I asked myself if this is how I wanted my first experience to be—having someone pay for it, no conversation, outside of any relationship? No, that's not how I wanted to move to this next stage of adulthood. But then I got to thinking: Why would I want to be a member of any group that would recruit members who would be favorably impressed by such an offer? Would I want to be one of their "brothers?" No thank you.

Yes, I needed to belong to something. All new college students do. I am sure my belonging needs were powerful. Not that I was thinking about that very intentionally and saying, "Hey, John, you've got to get on with meeting your belonging needs!" What was my college offering me in this regard? Fraternity rush, and not just trips to brothels. All six fraternities were inviting young men like me to parties and promising all the free beer we could consume. This was Ohio in 1961, and at age 18 one could purchase what was known as "3.2" (3.2% alcohol content)—very weak and cheap beer. But it was plenty potent stuff, as I was to learn my first year in college, not from consuming it myself, but from seeing and smelling the results of its impact on my fellow first-year students.

After rush week came the "bids," which were invitations delivered in writing to the lucky young men who were asked to join. I received two bids. One was from the brothers of Tau Epsilon Phi, which was known in the student culture as "the Jewish fraternity." I was Christian by family background, although no longer a real practicing Christian. This TEP fraternity was the only one of the six that did not have what used to be known as a "White Christian clause." I decided against joining any fraternity.

Not joining a fraternity meant I was ignoring my father's advice about the merits of doing so—which, by the way, was based on his belief, as he told me, that joining a fraternity was exactly like joining a company and learning how to lead that company. A lifetime mantra of his was, "Son, find a good company and stick with it." Joining a fraternity would have been just as I have seen that for so many other college graduates, is like joining a life-long "company." I didn't understand then what I understand now: Fraternity-affiliated males are more likely to experience bonding, affinity with other students, and loyalty to the institution than nonaffiliated males. Hence, they are more likely to graduate, to give more money to their alma mater, and to exercise more influence over these colleges as alumni.

Freshman Convocation: Setting Expectations Low

I have saved the worst part, not the best part, of orientation until last: the welcome convocation. I knew from my study of Latin in high school that the word *convocation* literally meant "to call together," as in a welcoming ceremony to college. Ours was held in the First Baptist Church of Marietta, which was immediately across from the main gate entrance to the campus. Initially, although I knew that Marietta represented itself as an "independent," "nondenominational" college, I didn't give a thought to the fact that we were being welcomed in a Christian church sanctuary. I was aware this was 1961 and that Marietta had disaffiliated itself officially from the Congregational Church in 1950, just 11 years previously.

Other than the location I remember only two things about the ceremony. The first was that this was my opportunity to personally experience one of the most time-tested, traditional, negative motivational messages in the 1,000-year history of Western higher education history: the famous "look to the left and look to the right" speech. There I was, a naïve, immature, reluctant 17-year old male, and my college president says from the altar podium: "Look to the left and look to the right . . . and the two students you just looked at won't be here when *you* graduate 4 years from now." I was an obedient student. I did as I was told. I looked at both of the students on either side of me and wished them a sad and silent farewell. And then I realized that they had each looked at me!

At the same time, I was looking and listening attentively to my president. He didn't look unhappy in the slightest about this extremely negative forecast about how many of us were and were not going to make it. To the contrary, he actually seemed both pleased and proud of this predicted outcome, like the purpose of the college experience was to get rid of many of us. And I set out to fulfill the president's prediction.

My other memory of that ceremony I owe to two fellow students who were filing out with me after the ceremony ended. I listened intently because I could hear they were complaining about the event. But their complaints were not directed at what was said, but where it was said, namely, in the sanctuary of the First Baptist Church. What was the problem? Both these students were Jewish and from New York City, and they had just discovered what we now call "buyer's remorse." What they thought they had purchased, a nonsectarian experience, was not what they were going to get at all. This conclusion would never have occurred to me at that time in life were it not for my openness to hearing the reactions from my fellow students to what we had all just experienced.

The Influence of Students in the First College Year

In addition to my fellow students on the crew team, whom I will write about later, I had several other experiences of even greater long-term impact involving the influence on me of other students.

Leaving College

I had been in college about 6 weeks and one day returned to my room to find my roommate packing a huge "steamer trunk," something all college kids had and brought to their residential college with all their worldly goods inside. He was packing everything he had into that huge trunk. Initially, I could only think that he was changing rooms because he no longer wanted to live with me. I had thought we had a decent relationship even though, very unlike me, he was a macho football player. At least he was a fellow New Englander like me, from Boston. Suddenly I had this thought, something clicked. I thought about how this guy had been mailing his dirty clothes home to Boston for his mother to launder for him and dutifully return to

Marietta. At times there were delivery delays, and he had totally exhausted his supply of clean clothes. Not good for a football player. As a historical note, in the early 60s this practice of college students mailing soiled laundry back home was so ubiquitous that the United States Postal Service actually stocked and sold boxes expressly for this purpose.

This guy and I had one thing in common, which we never spoke about: not sharing our feelings. I asked him what was going on, and he replied, "I am leaving college!" I was stunned. I didn't know one could just up and leave college. It was not one of the options my father had given me when he dropped me off to start college. But my roommate's statement kept ringing in my ears. Little did I know that later in my life and career one of my closest scholar colleagues in field of student retention, Vincent Tinto, would publish a book in 1987 entitled *Leaving College.* My roommate literally "wrote the book" on that 26 years before. In Vince's language this young man was neither "academically and socially integrated" into that college and hence was a ripe candidate for attrition. And I had the presence then to know that I wasn't "integrated" either and this young man could be me. What did I do? I helped him finish gathering his things, and then I trudged with him, helping him lug his heavy steamer trunk about a mile to the Greyhound bus station so he could catch the "Big Dog," the Greyhound bus, back to Boston. The Greyhound line was the only public transportation in and out of Marietta— then and now. I never heard from him again. But I know now that yes, students can and do leave college for all sorts of reasons, disproportionately for nonacademic reasons, and in this case failure to receive laundered clothes from his mother, a true proxy for homesickness.

Who did I get for my next roommate? Another kid from the Boston area who had earned the collegiate nickname of "Bunky." He had the ability to lie is his bed perfectly prone while he drank beer. Drink a lot of beer he did, and he spent a lot of time in bed. And he too left Marietta after the next semester, and I have never heard from him again either.

Developing Friendships for Life

In contrast, I had another friend, John Strance, who in the first semester of college became distraught when he learned that his parents had separated after he left for Marietta College. He too dropped out in the middle of the first semester, went back to his home in California, was totally unsuccessful in getting his parents back together, and thus returned to Marietta in the spring semester. It was only later in my career that I discovered that family disruption, especially decisions by parents to separate and divorce after the last child leaves home, is a predictable part of the first-year experience. John and I both had in common that we were children of privilege. We remained close until he died a few years ago. Thank goodness for lifetime friendships, a lasting effect of the undergraduate experience.

Saved by a Student

About halfway through my first term of college, I learned the truth of this now well accepted understanding that students powerfully influence other students. I was rescued by a sophomore, by which the Greeks meant "wise fool." To me this student was the wisest I met in college.

I was performing terribly in all five of my courses. One day after my political science American Government 101 class, a fellow student, Dan Berman, approached me and observed: "John, I notice you are not doing very well in this course. And I notice you are not taking any notes!" I acknowledged the accuracy of his observation and he proceeded to show me his notebook. And this was like asking any evangelical to discover the revealed word, which could be done by touching any page of the Bible. Every single page of Dan's notebook revealed his winning strategy of taking verbatim notes of the professor's lecture in his unique shorthand. This was in the era before any kind of recording device except human handwriting. I was amazed. Dan really had captured every word. He explained to me the following: (a) Most faculty create their exams by referring to what they had covered in class; hence if you had "good notes" you could recall everything a professor said in class; and (b) many students make the mistake while listening and taking notes of *not* writing down any repetition by the professor of key points. That is a terrible mistake. Why? Because repetition reveals those key points the professor thinks are most important, and hence, as Dan argued, those were most likely to be on the test. In addition, he showed me how he organized his notes, inserting margin summaries, callouts, and headings with key repetition of main points. I was amazed. I couldn't believe what I was being shown. But I decided that I couldn't possibly do any worse, so why not try to emulate my new friend Dan? I did that immediately, and my grades began to improve. Over the next few months, I became a world-class note taker. Other than literally going to class, that became my single most important study skill. I would never have thought of this were it not for Dan Berman, a fellow student. Marietta College did *not* have, in 1961, a first-year seminar, college success course, or learning center. We were all left to our own devices. It was truly sink or swim. Thus, the power of a fellow student was filling a huge vacuum in what should have been greater institutional responsibility for my success.

Dan remained my closest friend during the next 3 years until he graduated 1 year ahead of me. His enormous influence continued. I followed him to the same graduate school, Purdue University, for the same graduate program in American Studies. And years later after I had become a faculty member at USC, I recruited Dan to become a fellow faculty member. In 1989 I appointed him to become the codirector of USC's University 101 course, of which I was the executive director. Dan served in this capacity until he retired, and we remained the closest of friends and former colleagues until he died in September of 2021. I am certain had Dan not taught me how to take lecture notes that I would have flunked out and well, who knows? My life certainly would have turned out far differently than I can imagine.

What Does It Mean to Be "A Good Student"?

In the same course where I learned to take lecture notes, I had another lifelong influencing experience: discovering one definition of what it means to be a good student (and a good professor). One day at the conclusion of class, my professor, R. S. Hill, pulled me aside and asked, "Mr. Gardner, would you like to be a good student?" As context, this was after midterm, and I was failing his course. Naturally, I was unprepared for his question. I was living my life as someone who had never really considered how to be a good student. But more than any other professor in college, Professor Hill taught me that the questions are often more important than the answers, and that I had to get the questions right. My immediate response to his question was "Yes, sir, but how would I go about doing that?" His explanation: "Well, for starters, you need to keep yourself informed; and there is only one way to do this: read a good, daily, *national* newspaper." I asked, "What is a national newspaper?" He responded that there were really only three: "*The New York Times, The Washington Post*, and the *Los Angeles Times*." He did not mention *The Wall Street Journal*. But he did then add *The Christian Science Monitor*. Realizing that I was in Marietta, Ohio, not any of the places where these papers were published, I asked him, "How would I go about doing this, sir?" His response: "You would walk with me after class, right now, one block to People's Newsstand, and we would both get our papers. *The New York Times* comes in on the 11:22 a.m. Greyhound from Pittsburgh" (and our class had just let out at noon). He actually walked me down to that newsstand and showed me how I could pay the store 1 week in advance for a "reserved" paper held just for me. Thank you, Professor Hill and the messenger of civilization, the Greyhound, to Marietta, Ohio!

Professor Hill had also given me explicit reasons why I should be reading this paper:

- By doing so I would know exactly what U.S. and world leaders in government and business were reading and thinking about each day.
- Because *The Times* published the actual transcripts of major speeches and court opinions, I would be able to make up my own mind and interpretations of what a person had said and what that meant.

What he was really trying to get me to see was that this habit, should it become a habit, would make me more of an independent, informed, and critical thinker.

I discovered then one of the most important lessons about a successful first year of college: It is a period when we help students develop what can and should become lifelong habits for living, working, and citizenship. And in my own individual case, I finally was allowing myself to be liberated from my father's prejudice against *The New York Times*. He used to say it was a "communist-inspired paper," and he would never allow it in our home even though we lived only 50 miles out of New York City. Further, in my case, I would incorporate for years the required reading of *The Times* in my college courses at USC.

Academic Advising in My First Year of College

Unlike many first-year students, I actually got to meet with my academic advisor during orientation. We talked through my thinking about courses to take, and he failed to give me advice that would have kept me out of trouble, though—I need to own my choices and I do. But I didn't know then what I know now: how important those first course selections are when you are starting college.

I had to take English 101, of course. My professor never liked my writing style, so I could never earn more than a C on the weekly themes. On the final exam I wrote in the way I knew he wanted me too, and I received an A. But he still gave me a C for the course. Math was not a graduation requirement, so I skipped it. Not a smart move. I remain mathematically challenged to this day, having only mastered geometry and failing Algebra I in high school. I had to take a foreign language. I had done outstanding work in Latin in high school, but Latin wasn't offered at Marietta. I had also done well in French. But I thought I ought to do something different in college. That was a bad idea. I took Russian, or I should say it took me. My final grade was an F.

I had to take a science, so again I opted for something new instead of biology or chemistry. I had done satisfactory work in both courses in high school, but I really wasn't interested in them. I made another bad choice in deciding on geology. I got a C in the lecture, but an F in lab, which gave me an F for the course. Geology lab required memorizing over 400 different specimens of what I thought of generically as "rocks." I never could figure a way to remember them, and I absolutely hated the course. And there was American Government with Professor Hill. Thank goodness for my C. There was also Speech 101, which was a game changer (as I shall explain subsequently) in spite of my grade of D. I did get one A in the first semester—in physical education, an automatic A because I was playing a varsity sport (crew). And it was actually the only real challenge I rose to in the first term of college.

At midterm, my grades were three F's, two D's, and one A. My advisor's take on all this was as I reported previously: "Mr. Gardner, you are the stupidest kid I have ever advised!" Of course, I knew I wasn't doing well. And I knew I was only 17, lonely, homesick, lovesick, and bored with all my courses. But his feedback was still devasting. Was I the "stupidest kid," really? Could I be that bad? What could I do? Well, I made one smart move and got another academic advisor. What happened to my former advisor? He went on and became a college president in Texas! My new advisor was Kermit Gatten, a sociologist from whom I took a number of courses. He really opened up my head and let rational thinking and liberalism in and conventional religiosity out! As my advisor, he actually invited me to his home for dinner. I met his wife and children, and he advised me all the way through to graduation. He helped me make great decisions, especially about what courses I should take. He never tried to recruit me to his major, although I took enough sociology courses to have it be my major. Instead, I remained by choice an undecided student and received an interdisciplinary bachelor's degree with extensive coursework in history, political science, sociology, and English. I owe my academic advisor a big vote of thanks for getting me through college. He and I remained friends in regular communication until his death. Thank you, Kermit Gatten!

Reading as Punishment

The only course at my alma mater that no student could exempt, test out of, no matter what major, was Speech 101. Near the end of the term my professor approached me and informed me as follows: "Mr. Gardner, you know you have overcut this class and that your final grade should therefore be an F!" I acknowledged that I was aware of my "cuts" status. Six to be exact, which was three more than the allowable three. How had this happened? Love conquers all. I had cut both a Friday and a Monday class over three different weekends, which equals six cuts, all to drive back to New York City to see my girlfriend, whom I missed terribly. And, as I reported in the section on homesickness, I was exhibit A of what I learned from research on homesickness years later in my career: The more I went "home" to see the girlfriend, the more homesick I became. My professor introduced me to an age-old pedagogy, which we really need to practice more of today in college: extra reading assigned as punishment and penance. He offered me one of the most influential bargains of my life: "Mr. Gardner, how would you like to have a chance to get a D instead of an F, realizing that if you take the F you will have to repeat the course because a passing grade at any level in this course is a graduation requirement?" Without knowing what the "chance" might be, I leapt at it. "Mr. Gardner, you will then be required to read two books and stand an oral exam to measure what you learned from this reading. Is that acceptable to you?" I leapt at this too, without knowing what my reading experiences were to be. And he added: "And you better read every word of these books!"

A question: If you were to assign one of or all your students a reading that could be potentially life changing or influencing, what would you assign? And/or as you look back on your own college experience, did you read anything that you would describe as transformative in terms of its influence on your thinking and perhaps even life choices? My assignments were *Escape From Freedom*, by Erich Fromm, the German psychoanalyst who had escaped the Holocaust, and *The Lonely Crowd*, by David Riesman, attorney and Harvard University professor of sociology.

That speech professor was really wise. He had sized me up perfectly. I was an immature young man who was abusing my freedom in college by overcutting. And I was struggling to decide what kind of man I was going to become.

Escape From Freedom, which I read in 1961, again came to attention right after the election of Donald Trump in 2016. The work is an analysis by a survivor of the Holocaust about why the most liberal democracy in Europe in the 1930s (Germany), with the highest rate of literacy in Europe, voted in a totalitarian dictator and gave up the democracy of the Weimar Republic. Why do people give up their freedom? Why do they abuse the gift of the freedoms they enjoy and make poor choices (like overcutting six times)? Why is freedom such a hard thing to manage in life—like my freedom as a first-year student in college, or like many of my first-year fellow students who were giving up their freedom to be given orders by their fraternity and sorority big brothers and sisters? Why, as I would see after college, would millions of citizens relinquish their personal freedom for careers in the military? Bottomline: This one book really forced me to think about the behavioral choices I was making as a first-year student, choices that were not working out well for me at all!

The second work, *The Lonely Crowd*, while written originally for academics, also sold well to laypeople. Basically, its argument was that American society produced two types of citizens: "outer-directed" people and "inner-directed" people. My professor wanted me to see the choice was mine. What kind of person did I want to become? The vast majority of us are outer directed. We are constantly looking "out" at others to see what they think, do, wear, eat, and so on. Those persons are much more likely to be conformists and therefore more conventional in behaviors and chosen lifestyles and occupations. Contrastingly, the inner-directed person is more likely to be focused inward, concentrating on personal uniqueness in values, beliefs, goals. As I later learned, college professors are much more likely to be inner directed, which definitely is a perfect description of me! Riesman skillfully traced how American culture successfully socializes most of us to become outer-directed persons through advertising, media, social media, and even what we are given to read or be read to when we are children. It was Riesman's analysis of some of my favorite childhood books that helped me to see how I as a child had been socialized to become an outer-directed person and to "stay on track" in the American industrial and then postindustrial system of tracking people to our cultural definition of success. The combination of these two books really did a number on me. They had the effect of epiphany.

For my 30 years as a practicing professor at USC, I would always tell my students that one of my goals was to teach for epiphany. What I meant was that I was going to do my best to provide my students an experience consisting of ideas, information, and inspiration that would lead them—not me—to create epiphany. By this I mean arriving at a powerful insight, realization, or conclusion that transforms our previous thinking and leads us to actually do something, decide something, and take some action that, in turn, is transformative.

Both these books, thanks to just this one professor, provided me with catalysts for epiphany. They came at a time in my life when I was doing so badly in college that I had to decide what course of action I was going to pursue differently. What were the uses I was going to make of my freedom? Who and what was I going to allow myself to be influenced by? My answers to those questions led me to make choices for the rest of my college experience that changed me profoundly. Thank you, Professor Bernard Russi!

Getting On and Off Academic "Pro"

Academic probation, or "pro," was not a distinction that my parents wanted for me at the conclusion of my first term of college. Very simply, my grade-point average at the end of my first term was a 0.65 on a 3.0 scale. The requirement to continue in good academic standing was a 1.0, a C average. When Marietta College put a student on academic probation in 1961, it was just a notice of your academic classification. It did not entitle you, let alone provide you, with any kind of compensatory advising or academic support. It did not require you to take something like a college success course or study skills course. There was no mandatory reporting. There were no regular check-ins. You were on your own. All you knew was that if you didn't get your GPA up to a 1.0 by the end of the second semester, you were "outta there"! And this is exactly what academic probation means at hundreds of colleges and universities about 60 years later. It doesn't have to be, shouldn't be, structured this way. Thankfully, I got my second semester grades up to two A's, two B's, and a D (in Russian), but that was sufficient to get me off academic probation. And as a footnote, 13 years later when I was on the faculty at USC, I had the opportunity to teach an experimental course to help students who had been on probation and left the university and who were returning to college to be successful in their next attempt.

The First-Year Athletic Experience

I did join one group that had a huge impact on me, even though I was not a high performer in it: the crew team. In this respect I gave my father what he so desperately wanted. Never before had he been able to get me the slightest bit interested in organized, competitive sports. But crew? Well, crew was different—because there was no body contact, as in no hitting, blocking, fouling, or tackling another young man.

Crew was also unique because there were no heroes. No quarterbacks. In theory everyone on the team was equal. In an eight-oar "shell" every rower had to be perfectly in balance with all movements, in sync at all times with the other seven oarsmen, or else the shell was thrown off balance, which was the killer of forward movement speed that you had to maintain to win a race.

Because crew was a three-season sport, fall included some races, but the real season was spring. Winter was for conditioning, which in our Marietta winters, meant mainly running up and down the fieldhouse stairs for about an hour a day to build our leg muscles, the most important muscle group in the sport. In the spring we rowed 7 days a week. We started each day at 6:30 a.m. on the water for a 30-minute "time trial," which meant we rowed at full racing stroke. After that tremendous exertion, it was a real challenge to stay awake in morning classes. We then spent 3 hours every afternoon for a full practice on the river, no matter what the weather, and then ran a mile back to campus.

Besides coordination and teamwork, the sport was all about endurance. Tremendous physical exertion had to be sustained over varying periods depending on the length of the course, from as little as a mile, which, depending on wind and current, might be able to be done in 6 minutes, or a much longer course where we would be rowing at "racing stroke" for 25–30 minutes, a truly grueling experience. The sport took so much exertion that it was not uncommon for some oarspersons to vomit or pass out at the end of a race. It was explained to me that at racing stroke you are performing at the same rate as if you were lifting more than 50 pounds over your head 40–45 times a minute. How did you prepare for that level of exertion? Practice, practice, practice. Conditioning, conditioning, conditioning. Most commonly by running, preferably up steep stairs.

Crew was not a fair-weather sport. You usually went out on the water and rowed no matter what the weather. And when your oar handle would get wet in inclement weather, unless you had "taped" your hands, the unfinished wood on the blade would rub the skin on your hands raw and remove it.

Why did we do this? As I suggested, partially because of the beauty of the surroundings. And especially because of the beauty of the synchronicity of the human machine that we were a part of. And because of the power of the team—one for all, all for one. We never believed we could perform at this level until we found we could. In these respects, it became a metaphor for my college experience and life itself.

I was truly moved by my student-athlete experience, all in my attempt to please my father. But as my 2 years wore on as a "student" athlete on the crew team, I found that crew was a jealous lover. The sport demanded my highest allegiance and priority, and I decided I could no longer give it my all. Instead, I decided that one thing mattered even more: being an outstanding student. Rowing required a great deal of restorative sleep, and I needed to be studying in that sleep time in order to be a high-performing student academically.

Things I Didn't Do the First Year Because They Weren't Required

I didn't choose a major because we didn't have to do that at Marietta—ever! We were allowed to pursue a bachelor's degree with what was called a "division of concentration" in the hard sciences, social sciences, or humanities. This was, in effect, a custom-designed degree with no fixed major requirements other than the core curriculum requirements. And that's exactly what I did, but I'm not sure I would do it again. I realized in my senior year when I took four English courses that had I done this in my first year I might have become an English major. But by not declaring a major I was able to take almost as much history, political science, and sociology; my three heaviest fields of concentration, as I would have been able to do had I majored in any one of them, plus I was about to include 18 hours of English beyond English 101 and 102. And what did this prepare me to do? As it turned out, this actually prepared me to do a great deal.

I didn't find a romantic relationship either because I kept the one I had when I came to college for another 2 years. In retrospect, this was a great mistake. Having the same girlfriend over 3 years prevented me from having a more normal social life during college and from making any serious effort to get to know women as people, thinkers, doers, beyond the conventional gender-role stereotypes of that era. I didn't join even an informal group of drinking buddies, because I did not "drink" in the collegiate sense of that term to ensure that I would not become an alcoholic like my mother. Nor did I join any other clubs or student organizations for the first 2 years. Hence, you could say I was not very "involved" or "engaged" out of class.

My First Year of College in Sum

I did much, much better academically in my second semester and was able to get off academic probation. I attribute my improved academic performance to these factors: (a) some maturation on my part; (b) the profound influence of my teaching faculty in the spring term; (c) the continuing influence of my undergraduate student mentor, Dan Berman, whose lecture note-taking instruction really turned me around and who helped me identify faculty who would be a much better fit for me; (d) my new and outstanding academic advisor; (e) making better use of my college-given personal freedoms and thus making better decisions; and (f) abatement of the symptoms of acute homesickness.

But that miserable start ensured that no matter how well I did for my next seven semesters, my first semester GPA was a curse, a life sentence. It is mathematically impossible to pull up a 0.65 GPA and be admitted to Phi Beta Kappa (Marietta has the 16th oldest Phi Beta Kappa chapter in the United States). And I could never qualify for magna cum laude or even cum laude. My grades were magna level essentially from second semester on, but no matter. I have reflected that it would have been easier for me to have been pardoned in the state of Ohio for committing a felony than to have those first-term grades expunged. Marietta College had no formal system for what we now call "academic forgiveness."

Most people, of course, build a successful adult life on their strengths. It would seem that I have built a successful professional life on my first-year weaknesses, not my strengths. Those weaknesses almost trumped. Often today when I do professional presentations on the importance of the first year, I lay out arguments for why the first year matters. You would think we academics are already well aware of that. But we aren't, and many of us never even give that any consideration. My professional life has been devoted to trying to make the first year matter—more than it has for so many students. As the creator of the "first-year experience," I can truthfully say that my Marietta College experience was my experiential basis for my professional work to improve the first year of college. And I am pleased to report that the first year of college today at my alma mater is nothing like it was for me. To understate the reality, Marietta now does all kinds of things to support students that it didn't offer in the 1960s or do for me. I am so proud of my alma mater in this regard. And in spite of my own adversities in my first year, I am truly grateful for all it taught me about what a successful first-year experience needs to include. I did not know at the end of my first year or even when I graduated that I would make a life's work out of my initial failures at Marietta, and that is where the rest of this book is going.

For chapter discussion questions, click the link or scan the QR code to visit Appendix C of the Online Compendium.

https://styluspub.presswarehouse.com/uploads/5e35cd13add3605ede5537f a2a5159aac11d5b57.pdf

2

THE SECOND YEAR
OF COLLEGE

Continuing Recovery From the First Year

So often it is the things that happen to and for students that are not planned or officially sanctioned by the institution that matter most for student learning, engagement, and commitment. When I reflect on my sophomore year, I conclude that there were three experiences I had totally outside the formal curriculum that were most significant for me.

Finding Spaces for Community: The Cuban Missile Crisis of 1962

One of the many things I observe when visiting a campus is where students find space to congregate, to interact, meet new people, reflect, find solace, security, and comfort. A few years ago, I visited a community college out in Iowa where the president told me how proud he was of the absolutely spotless floors in the corridors of his buildings. I felt like I was back on active duty again in the Air Force in the hospital where I was stationed listening to my hospital commander praise the cleanliness of his facility. And it was truly spotless. We could have eaten off those floors. But the place I was visiting was not a hospital. It was a college campus where students like to gather and talk and study and think. This same president told me that after he became president he had any and all types of furniture in the hallways removed (such as chairs) so there were totally unobstructed views of the corridors and egress. Hmmm. You can guess what this made me wonder about. No thought had been given to spaces for student community.

Another place I visited a few years ago—an elite private, residential college in Pennsylvania—provided me a student-led tour of the campus. My guide was a graduating senior. As we leisurely walked the campus, he told me about the major life decisions he was facing: go to graduate school or to work; stay with his girlfriend after college and go to the same graduate school as she; or take a very lucrative engineering starting job, which would force him to geographically separate from her. I asked him what kinds of places there were on campus where he could go and either be alone or with others that would be ideal for reflection, contemplation, deep thinking, and/or serious conversation. He told me that he couldn't identify any. As we continued our walk around, we passed an imposing Gothic-like structure that he identified as the chapel. I asked him if he ever attended anything there. No was his reply. He told me he had never even entered that space. I suggested we do so together, and we did. I told him to just sit down and start thinking. Then I left him to his thoughts, reminding him he had a number of important decisions to make.

At Marietta both on and off the campus we were blessed with all kinds of suitable spaces for community and reflection. One of them was the very large lounge area in my sophomore residence hall. This was before college students had TVs in their rooms. The most likely place for community was in that lounge where there was the only television in the building. In October of 1962 almost every student in our building was in that room glued to the tube. Why? The United States was in a diplomatic and military stand-off with Russia over Russia's shipment to Cuba of ballistic missiles targeting the United States, and all of us were of draft age. That crisis went on for over a week, and we all spent more time in that room than anywhere else. But after the crisis was resolved, we didn't stop gathering there. We had gotten in a habit and the lounge met a need.

My Coming Out as a Campus Provocateur

It was March of 1963 and we were experiencing one of the greatest floods of the Ohio River in the town of Marietta in the 20th century. The waters had surged above flood stage and were literally lapping at the edge of the campus. One night during this flood, a taxicab made a turn on to a side street adjacent to the residence hall where I lived. The driver soon saw that the street was blocked by the flood water. He made a poor decision about where to make a last-minute hasty U-turn, in the greenway in the back of the hall. He quickly became mired in the mud. Not being able to spin or rock himself free, he got out of his car and walked over to our residence hall. I was observing all this from one of the four floors of the building, all of which had outdoor corridors that overlooked the field where this guy was stuck, like an old Holiday Inn. I saw him headed for the dorm and went down several flights to greet him in our lobby. Here I was, a privileged, preppy-looking college kid, and here was this guy not much older than I was but definitely working class and in a jam. He asked me if I could help him and round up some guys to help push him out. My dorm mates had other plans for him. So instead of volunteering to help, they volunteered to harass. They proceeded to throw food, water balloons, and water-filled condoms at him and his vehicle. They hurled verbal epithets at this poor guy. Someone set up a record player on one of the outside ramparts and began playing circus music. I made a foray out into the grassy morass to offer to let him use a phone in our hall's office. The poor guy was distraught. He couldn't believe these college boys had made his misfortune into an object of derision and entertainment and that no one would come out and help him. He explained to me that he would surely lose his job over this incident. I went back in the hall and tried again in vain to get anyone to help him. Meanwhile the taunting of the driver increased in intensity, as did the barrage of objects being hurled at him and his vehicle. Across the street was a female residence hall from which now women's voices were joining the male cacophony. I finally went into the hall office and called the police.

After several hours of retreating in my room, ruminating on my ineffectiveness to get any help for this fellow human being, I realized I just couldn't stand being in this environment any longer, at least that night. I packed a bag, walked the mile or so to the Greyhound bus station, and took a late-night bus up to Pittsburgh for a change to New York City. And I spent a full week there in an apartment owned by the mother of one my friends. She was wealthy; she and her husband had four residences, one of them being that apartment in New York City, which they weren't occupying that week. Why did I go to New York? Because that was where my girlfriend was in college. What a way to have a week's escape.

But I could not put out of my mind the incident that had driven me to flee the campus and look for sanctuary in New York City in the arms of my girlfriend. This moved me to write a letter to the editor of the college's student newspaper, *The Marcolian*. Because of time elapsed the letter was published the day before I returned to campus. This was a small college, 1,500 students or so, and we all read the campus rag. When I returned, many of my fellow students had read my letter in which I had taken to task my fellow dorm residents and tried to shame them. But they shunned me instead upon my return. However, my professors, and some of the students who didn't know me, really wanted to know just who is this John Gardner person? In truth, while I didn't know it at that time, this was my "coming out." I had taken a very public stand and challenged the norms and behaviors of the peer group with whom I lived. And people never looked at me the same way again. Literally, I was now expected to speak up and be heard and noticed. Expectations do indeed influence behavior. Several years ago, my wife and I went to the 50th reunion of the class of '65, and she and I went down into the basement of the college library where the archives are found. And I retrieved that letter, which I had not seen for over 50 years. Here is what I had written as a 19-year-old sophomore:

THE MARCOLIAN

MARCH 15, 1963

MAILBOX

Dear Editor:

Thursday evening, Mar 7, a man driving a cab owned by the New Cab Co. of Marietta, turned into Butler Street from Seventh Street and coming upon the water, which still covered the road, he foolishly entered the field along the road and attempted to make a "U" turn.

Having half completed his circle, he was halted by the mud. This was soon noticed by someone on a concourse of Men's Residence # 2 and as a few more men became aware of the cab in the field they began to yell.

These few yelling drew more men out and within a matter of several minutes, a large percentage of the dorm's 192 men were on the concourses mocking the cab driver in his efforts to get his vehicle free from the mud.

Despite the mass verbal encouragement and aid as well as accompanying recorded circus music and trumpeting, the driver could not move the cab. Furthermore, the cab driver's efforts were illuminated for the amusement of the spectators by a student-directed spotlight.

The driver eventually got out of his car, and immediately the heckling unanimously increased in intensity; and finally, when he was a few yards away from the dorm he was welcomed by cries of "HOOPEE*—SPIT ON HIM---SPIT ON HIM" and unprintable vulgarities.

He asked for no help from Men's Residence # 2 and none was offered. He reached his brother on the telephone who in a few minutes arrived in his Jeep and succeeded in pulling the cab out of the field.

Meanwhile the women in the dormitories across the street were flashing lights and cheering the men on. However, they did not stop their encouragement after the cab was gone. The men having already acted as a mass with the encouragement of the women became a mob and stampeded into the street as animals would and in a frenzy yelled "PANTY RAID, PANTY RAID."

Although their numbers swelled, there was no leader. A mass action had been accomplished, a mob action had not, but it was not due to lack of potential.

Now on the basis of these incidents, how do the residents of these particular buildings justify their actions? How do they justify them in light of their Christian ideals which preach brotherhood, respect for others, and help for those brothers in need?

How can they justify the emotional and frenzied actions as students in an institution of higher education, where, theoretically, they are attempting to confront situations intelligently, objectively, and maturely?

And how according to the moral code of our western culture, which maintains the dignity of the individual, can the students of Marietta College justify their destruction of one man's dignity and their own consequent self-degradation?

And finally, in light of these student actions, how does Marietta College justify the following statement found on the rear cover of every Marietta College Bulletin, "Marietta College has been dedicated to the task of helping our nation prepare young people to become intelligent, useful members of society. It further seeks to develop new leaders for a Christian democracy....?"

John N. Gardner

Men's Residence # 2

Note: "Hoopee" was a derogatory term, used by Marietta College students, to describe local Marietta residents based on the period of the town's founding in the late 18th century when a thriving local industry was barrel making. The steel "hoops" for the barrels were sent down the Ohio River from Pittsburgh, and the locals would be seen coming into town in their wagons to pick up their "hoops" for the barrels they would then make and, in turn, ship back up the river.

Taking Action to End Racial Discrimination in College Housing

Several months later I had another experience on my journey to become an equity warrior. This was definitely *not* part of the formal plan the college had for students like me. This was occasioned by the annual sign up for residence hall space for the following year. I had been in conversation with what the college officially called a "foreign student," one Benjamin Davies, who was from Liberia. He had come to an American college to major in prelaw in order to go to a U.S. law school. His country's legal system had been greatly influenced more than a century before by our legal system, and especially our Constitution. I had met this guy in one of my political science courses. Both of us put each other down as a requested "suitemate" for one of the suites of eight, which was the configuration of this hall. Eventually, I received an official communication from the college's office of the dean of men (a vestigial organism no longer found in most U.S. institutions along with its analog, the dean of women). The notice informed me that my housing request assignment had been denied. My friend, Ben Davies, received the same communication.

Wasting no time, I marched myself in to see the chief housing officer, the dean of men, John Sandt. I asked him for an explanation as to why my roommate request had been denied. He very candidly told me he was actually doing me a "big favor." Incredulously, I asked what he meant by that. He told me that he was just looking after me and that I would not be happy living with this student. He went on to say that such students had different personal habits around personal hygiene and that it was his policy to house "foreign" students in their own facility. He didn't use the words "separate" let alone "segregated," but I understood the code. And this was a year before the Civil Rights Act. What could I do? I went to the library and asked for help. I had a favorite librarian, a very helpful and compe- tent French woman, Lou Gould, who, I had discovered previously, could help me find anything. I just loved interacting with her. She took me into the government documents section and helped me find some documenta- tion to support my contention that the college was in violation of federal law. I then made an appointment to see the college president. I put on a Brooks Brothers suit I almost never wore at college, and I got straight to the point: "President Duddy, you have a dean of men who is—and there- fore *you* are—practicing racial discrimination in housing assignments. We are a residential liberal arts college, and this kind of practice violates our academic integrity and the law." He got the point that a well-dressed student was threatening to take legal action against the college. He pro- fessed ignorance of such a policy but promised me that I would get my requested suitemate and that separate housing for international students would stop. And it did.

What did I learn from this?

- One person could make a difference—in this case, the president, the dean of men, and two individual students, the latter one White American, one Black African, both of whom just wanted to be roommates.

- Information is power. The information I got in the campus library with our professional librarian allowed me to present an evidence-based case for change.
- A system can be changed. It often takes threat of forced change, but it can happen reasonably, peacefully, and within the system.
- I didn't have to accept the status quo, and I could be a positive force for change.
- I will be more effective if I work within the system.
- Institutionalized racist policies can and must be changed.

And so my sophomore year ended. I was no longer a "wise fool," which was the original Greek meaning for this term. I had made my presence felt on a small college campus, which was proving to me to be a relatively risk-free laboratory environment where I could test out how to act like an adult. The school year ended, and I went back to Connecticut and almost immediately back to work again in "the Can," the term United Steelworkers of America, such as I was in the summers, gave to the Hillside, New Jersey, plant of the American Can Company. This continued to be a profound but different kind of learning experience from college for me.

For chapter discussion questions, click the link or scan the QR code to visit Appendix C of the Online Compendium.

https://styluspub.presswarehouse.com/uploads/5e35cd13add3605ede5537f
a2a5159aac11d5b57.pdf

3

THE THIRD YEAR
OF COLLEGE

Making Some Successful Decisions

M ajor milestones in college include making good decisions, one day at a time, realizing that all are cumulative in their integrated impact. This was a year for

- deciding on what would be my first priority: sports, a romantic relationship, or my academic progress
- taking a chance on doing something real men weren't supposed to do
- accepting a personal loan and repaying it initially and then later in life when it really made a difference
- giving my only class presentation in 4 years of college
- being shaped by one of America's greatest national tragedies
- discovering the most important value on which my future life's work would be based—a discovery made squarely in the curriculum
- learning more about how to unsuccessfully challenge the status quo
- being mesmerized by the concept of "the banality of evil"
- emancipating myself from a constraining relationship

All of these influence me to this very day.

Some college students reach a point in college when they have to decide if they going to commit themselves to doing what they have to do to be really good students. That was how I started my junior year.

I made one decision that would provide a framework for the year, my first attempt to more or less live with a woman in a relationship. I had "gone steady" with this person for the 2 previous years and had missed her greatly while I was away at college. She was ahead of me in college and had graduated from a Catholic school in New York City with an education degree that permitted her to teach in parochial schools. She got an elementary school teaching job in a Catholic school in Parkersburg, West Virginia, 13 miles down the river from Marietta, Ohio, where I was a college student. My parents were furious about this development. Their response: cutting my allowance by 50%. Her parents weren't happy about it either. Both sets of parents agreed they didn't want their children getting married outside the faith, and mine were particularly concerned that my partner would get pregnant and ruin my college experience and therefore, life chances.

I had decided by the end of my sophomore year that I loved the "student part" of being a college student. And I wanted to get even better at that. I was discovering my own passion for the life of the mind. I knew that if the young woman moved close to me, the relationship was going to be a significant time commitment and that the rest of my time just had to go to my studies. And there was my crew team slot. Crew was tremendously demanding. It was a three-season, 7-day-a-week commitment. And it demanded a great deal of sleep just to function athletically. I just didn't see how I could do crew justice and commit to my courses and my girlfriend, so I gave up the crew team. My father was really upset about this. I was not supposed to be a "quitter." He would have been perfectly fine if I had been a gentleman C student but a full-time varsity lightweight oarsman. Now that was real preparation for adult life. But that was not to be. I gave up crew cold turkey. And that year I made 11 A's and one B. Now I have to tell you about that one B.

Doing Something Real Men Didn't Do

I confess the following with some embarrassment: I avoided a true science course in favor of home economics! In college I was a true STEM-phobic student. After failing geology in my first year, I still had to complete 8 hours of a laboratory science. I took another stab at fulfilling this graduation requirement by returning to a discipline in which I had done reasonably well in high school, although without enthusiasm: chemistry. And there I discovered one of the most enthusiastic professors for one's own discipline of my entire career. This was Professor Gross, the department chair who described himself as a corporate refugee to the academy giving up his former life as a Dupont research chemist. He truly loved being in class every day and never failed to tell us so. And responding in kind, I actually did pretty well, by my standards, with a B. But I still lacked the courage to risk taking a second STEM course, attributing my B to one-time luck and Professor Gross. I had to take something for the last 4 credits I needed of laboratory science. Thanks to my resourceful and knowledgeable academic advisor, I learned that home

THE THIRD YEAR OF COLLEGE   *37*

economics and its "Principles of Food Preparation," four-credit course, was classified as a lab science. So off I went. I found myself the only male in a class of 28 women. Yes, they gave me funny looks, and I could only imagine what they were thinking about my norm-breaking presence. My instructor also learned of my rationale for being in her course, and she was not pleased by my using this as a means of avoiding a real science. This made her even more exacting of my performance in the two 3-hour labs a week.

In one of the labs, a Monday before the Thanksgiving break, the assignment was to bake a loaf of bread from scratch. I failed. My dough never rose. My instructor insisted I come back on the following lab day, the Wednesday before Thanksgiving, with the result that I was the only student in the lab. But this time the dough did rise, and I took the loaf home to my family for Thanksgiving dinner. However, because I had to stay over another whole day to fulfill this assignment, I missed my ride back east, and my parents had to fly me back home, which made this loaf of bread the most expensive one in the family history!

In another lab focused on making desert sauces I ruined a double-boiler pan by cooking the sauce too long. My professor was disgusted. In truth, if it hadn't been for all my new female friends, I would never have been able to pass the lab portion of the course. As for the lecture portion, I had the highest grades in the class. I really could memorize those recipes. But the A in lecture had to be balanced out with the performance in lab, which at best had to be a C, if that, and this reduced my final grade to my only B, looking very conspicuous now on my college transcript along with the 11 A's for that year. In truth I actually enjoyed the class, solely due to the camaraderie with the women. They were much more collaborative and noncompetitive than a class of men would have been. They actually listened to me and asked me interesting questions, which I reciprocated. During every class I felt that I was one of them and that all the gender differences I had learned were totally irrelevant to what we were doing together. I believe I was a somewhat different student after this course. My gender identity had been shifted in some way I did not yet fully understand (another impact of college?).

Accepting A Gift That Required No Repayment: The Transformative Power of Giving

I mentioned earlier that one of the constraints I had to contend with in my junior year was reduced financial circumstances. As a child of now reduced privilege, my allowance had been reduced from $100 to $50 per month because of my father's disapproval of my choice for a romantic relationship.

As he told me many times, "Son, I don't pay for what I don't approve of!" This really left me in hard times. Therefore, I did the unthinkable for a kid from my background: I got a job during the academic term! In my undergraduate era I knew very few students who "worked" during the school year. This was pre-1965 Higher Education Act, so there was no federally funded student financial aid/work study, which I wouldn't have qualified for anyway. The "job" I got was as a student assistant for 15 hours per week in the college library. I learned the mantra that "a mis-shelved book is a lost book." While this position helped my cash flow, it was a huge distraction from what I wanted to do the most: study. And I was in a constant state of panic about not having enough time to be the really good student I aspired to be. After doing this a month or so, I received in the mail a crisp $50 bill from a wealthy woman who was the mother of one of my friends. I told her about having to take a job at college. She disapproved, and she told me that I should never be without an emergency $50 in my wallet. She encouraged me to quit my job and told me that she would henceforth send me a check for $50 every month for the rest of the year or until my full allowance was restored. She added that I should consider this a gift not expected to be repaid, but that someday in the future I should do the same for some other deserving person in need.

What did I do? Well, I'll tell you what I didn't do: inform my parents. What I did do was quit my job. I also resolved to repay this nonloan, and to do the same for someone else in the future. In the very next summer after my junior year, I sold my car and took the proceeds and repaid what had amounted to a $450 intended gift. My benefactor never acknowledged the check, but she did cash it. By the end of my junior year, I didn't know what I wanted to do, but I knew I wanted to have enough money to practice philanthropy even if it was at a modest level. And 3 years later when I was on active duty in the Air Force, I discovered someone worthy of my returning that gift.

I am getting a bit ahead of myself here in writing about my military experience, but I want to close off this lesson on the power of gifting to others. Just after I arrived at my permanent duty station, Shaw AFB in Sumter, South Carolina, at age 22, I made the acquaintance of a remarkable, young, enlisted man, Airman Raymond Booth. I learned he was one of 10 children from a rural Ohio family. His father was a steelworker, and no one in the family had ever been to college. This kid was so bright. He was incredibly gifted as a humorist—and I had learned that true humor has to be based on keen underlying intelligence and verbal facility. I thought to myself "this guy just has to go to college," so I talked to him about doing so. His response: "No, I couldn't possibly do that; no one in my family ever has, and besides I don't have the money." Actually, it didn't take much money as the Air Force would pay 75% of the tuition for college courses offered on base if the troop paid the other 25%. Raymond claimed he didn't have even the 25%, and I believed him. I said: "OK, Booth, what happens if the 25% consideration goes away and you didn't have the money as an excuse?" He allowed he wouldn't be left with any excuse. I told him I would give him the 25% for the first course to see how being a college student felt to him. He did well, and I paid for three more courses, by which time he was shipped to Okinawa. He continued his college course-taking on his own; returned to the States after his honorable discharge; finished a bachelor's and a master's degree; and taught Ohio middle school kids social studies for 30 years. I was and am so proud of him. We talk at least monthly to this day. Even as a young man I had discovered the wonderful act of investing in others through "giving." All this was launched by my own college experience.

One Class Presentation in 4 Years

I was a college student in the all-lecture all-the-time pedagogical era. I must confess I was an auditory learner who eventually thrived in the lecture-dominated classroom. And, thankfully, I had many excellent lecturers at Marietta whom I genuinely loved listening to. When I became a college teacher myself, they were truly my role models, the gold standard for what I thought I was expected to do. There was only one course I took out of my 40 or so over 4 years of undergraduate education where I was required to "speak," and that was my very influential Speech 101 class, as I have reported on previously. I did a class presentation in only one other course. But in contrast, in my other 38 courses, while there were occasional class discussions, I was never required to give an actual prepared class presentation.

The one presentation I gave was so rare, so much the exception, that I will remember it for the rest of my life. In fact, my memory now over 50 years later is so vivid that I could give that presentation right now. I'm not exaggerating! To spare you, I won't. As it had developed, this one-time learning experience was not one the professor had planned on or incorporated into his syllabus. This was Professor Eugene Murdock, a political historian, and the course was American Political Parties. At some point in the course, we were focusing on the practice in the pre–Voting Rights Act era of the American South, and Professor Murdock was tracing the legal route to the famous *Brown v. Board of Education* 1954 case that struck down the infamous "separate but equal" provision established in the 1896 *Plessy v. Ferguson* case. One of the key cases along the way was *Smith v. Allwright*, 1944, which overturned the long-standing practice of the so-called "White primary."

When the professor cited this case, out of curiosity I asked him on what basis the Supreme Court had struck down this long-standing practice? In what became a model for my own subsequent teaching, Professor Murdock informed the class he did not know the answer to my question. But as a gifted teacher, he responded: "Mr. Gardner, why don't you look into this question and come back and report your findings to the class?" Of course, I was surprised but felt that I had no choice but to do as he asked. A week later I was prepared to answer my own original question and make my presentation. I cannot remember the reactions of my fellow students, but I can remember my professor's and my own. Professor Murdock was very pleased and complimentary. I was thrilled and amazed I could do it ("it" being the actual presentation, not the research to prepare to deliver it). What strikes me now as so significant is that it was a reflection of the dominant pedagogy of that era in that even in a small, liberal arts college with very small classes, the norm was that we students were to be talked at, not heard from. The practice of what we would now call "active learning" had not yet come into vogue. It would be my hope that the students at my readers' institutions get to do more than one or two presentations over the course of an undergraduate degree. We must do better than this to prepare students for "the real world!"

One other important learning in this American Political Parties course was as a result of being required to read the 1949 book by one of the most important 20th-century thinkers in political science, V.O. Key, and his book *Southern Politics in State and Nation*. Of course, I had no idea at the time this was assigned to me that I would ultimately be sent involuntarily by the U.S. Air Force to the American South and then decide voluntarily to live my adult career and life there. What really stuck with me in reading Key's book, as reinforced by our professor, was that to understand essentially anything of significance in southern politics (and I would add now education) the role of race must be considered as having significant underlying contextual influence. As both V.O. Key and my professor emphasized: Race underlies all considerations in life and politics in the South.

Memorable Global Events That Influenced Me

As a child growing up, I lost track of all the times I heard my father recall where he was on December 7, 1941, what he was doing, and how he reacted to the news of the bombing of Pearl Harbor. To hear him tell the story, he was in a football stadium. He heard, literally, President Roosevelt's voice over the public address system and wanted to rush out and enlist the very next day. But he couldn't because he was a plant manager of a factory that needed to be converted immediately to the manufacture of war materials.

My equivalent to Pearl Harbor was November 22, 1963, and the assassination of President Kennedy. I too remember where I was and what I was doing. I was in Professor Hill's Political Philosophy course at about 1:45 p.m. on that warm, late fall day. The windows were open, and we could hear some student commotion, animated talking, going on outside the building. Soon the class was interrupted by a student who burst in and announced: "The president has been shot!" Of course, I didn't know it yet, but this was to be one of the truly defining occasions of my generation and my college experience. Our professor dismissed the class immediately. Students were congregating everywhere and talking about one subject as they never had before. I tired of this eventually and sought my place of solace and sanctuary on campus: the library. And I was almost the only student in the place. I went to the card catalogue and then to other sources to see what I could find written by President Kennedy. Of course, this was all pre-internet, but as a budding historian I understood and appreciated the importance of going to the primary source. I spent hours poring over his speeches, as if that could bring him back to life.

His murder took place on the Friday before our Thanksgiving vacation was to commence the following Wednesday. Now President Johnson announced that day that Monday was to be observed as a national day of mourning. That would leave us with only Tuesday classes before our holiday break. The college administration recognized that because we now had a free Monday many students would just cut the Tuesday classes. The decision was made and announced that there would be no more classes before Thanksgiving, hence the murder of our president was an occasion for an extended holiday. I was stunned that our college leadership was so insensitive. But I became even more stunned by the reaction of my fellow students. They were overjoyed. Pandemonium broke loose in the residence hall; shouting, cheering, and immediate rush to alcohol-fueled celebration. I was appalled and disgusted and reminded once again that I wasn't really like most of my fellow students at all.

We know now, after decades of research, that many college students are influenced by the president: what the president says, does, stands for, and presents as fundamental values and beliefs. President Kennedy had attracted my attention even before college. In retrospect, I was moved most by his global orientation and his belief in the importance of people who were more fortunate giving back in service, as in, most notably, the Peace Corps and

VISTA (Volunteers in Service to America). While I was not as self-aware as I am today, he, President Kennedy, as a man from privilege, had inspired me, a child of privilege. That lesson has been lifelong. I was one of those kids for whom President Kennedy's inaugural words, "Ask not what your country can do for you; ask what you can do for your country," had really been heard and absorbed. While I didn't have a clue yet what I could do for my country, I knew by the day of his death that I had to do something, was going to do something, and that Marietta College was helping me think this through. I firmly believe today that the single most important role of college needed for our democracy in the third decade of the 21st century is to produce graduates to do "something!"

Beginning My Search for Justice

Ideally, some of the most important things that happen to undergraduate students are those that arise out of the curriculum. This was certainly true in my case, with almost equal time and credit given to all that I learned outside the curriculum, in what we now call "the cocurricular experience." As I reflect on my undergraduate curriculum the following courses had the greatest impact on me:

- in my first year, Speech 101, because public speaking is now something I do for a living and because of the influence of the two books I was forced to read as punishment, as I described previously
- also in my first year, Sociology 101, which absolutely transformed my understanding of the influence of group membership on individual behaviors and destroyed any conventional religious beliefs I had
- in my junior year, Political Philosophy and the beginning of my lifelong search for an answer to the question "What is justice?"
- in my senior year, an English course on the transcendental period of 19th-century U.S. literature for exposing me to the inspiration of Ralph Waldo Emerson and his call for "self-reliance" and introducing me to the intellectual inspiration of other so-called "transcendental" period of writers

But to return to my junior year, I received my greatest inspiration for an idea that would become the basis for my life's work: the meaning and pursuit of justice.

The course was Political Philosophy with my influential professor and *New York Times* advocate, R.S. Hill. In this course we read probably 20 different political philosophers from ancient, medieval, Renaissance, colonial, and contemporary times, both U.S. and European. But the work that stuck with me the most was Plato's *Republic* and its narrated journey of a philosopher (Socrates) in search of truth and the meaning of justice. First, I was struck by the philosopher's method of intellectual inquiry, one I have often pursued as an adult, namely through verbal dialogue in the interrogatory mode. Socrates's ultimate discovery of his answer to the questions of "What is justice?" and "Who should rule?" (His answer to the latter—philosopher kings) had these influences on me:

- The question of "What is justice?" would become the most important for me to answer in my life's work, namely the pursuit of justice for first-year college students—the outcome of which would determine who would get more—and less—justice in American life.
- The primary means to discover the meaning and pursuit of justice would come through working and communicating collaboratively with other thinkers and doers to determine their answers to the question of what is justice for first-year college students, and hence my work in founding "The First-Year Experience."
- Everyone has a personal notion of the truth, and it is incumbent upon all educated persons to develop their own notions of the truth, which are created by adding up and borrowing from the half-truths of others.
- The questions raised in a good college education and ultimately in life may be more important than the answers. Therefore, one has to get the questions right.

Ironically and coincidentally, Professor Hill, as he was leading us through the explication of Plato's thinking, reached the point of revealing Plato's answer to the question for all human societies of "Who should rule?" on the very afternoon that President Kennedy was murdered.

Why am I relating all this about Plato's *Republic* and the meaning of justice? Because this was the *big idea* out of my whole college experience. I discovered this in one course, at the hands of one professor, in my junior year. I was, admittedly, a searcher on a journey of intellectual and personal discovery. I was developmentally ready for this. I was looking for some guiding principle/idea that would provide me a foundation for lifelong work as an adult. Admittedly, I still didn't know what I was going to do with this. But now I was much more ready to make these ultimately important life choices. Thank you, Professor Hill. Thank you, Marietta College.

Learning How Not to Challenge the Status Quo of Fraternity Life: Being "Stonewalled"

One of the things that had happened to me in my junior year was the result of my intolerance of the so-called "Greek"-letter social fraternities and sororities. Part of the reason for my attitude was my rejection of my father's value system, which had led him to join and thrive in a fraternity at Dartmouth College. As I have related previously, during my first year in college I had decided not to join a fraternity. But as my college years progressed, I became more militant about my disdain for what I had understood were the hallmarks of fraternal life. And so, I set out on a campaign with another student, Dan Berman, previously described as my note-taking mentor, to discredit and urge the abolition of Greek life at Marietta College. In truth, I especially directed my ire to fraternities, not sororities. But how naïve I had to have been to think for a minute I could successfully take on these hugely influential groups.

What were the bases of my objections to fraternity life?

- I was opposed to their exclusionary membership practices based on so-called "White Christian" membership restrictions.
- I was appalled by the ritualized hazing practices to which I observed them subjecting fellow students. Such hazing kept students sleep deprived, constantly intoxicated, and unbathed, and disrupted what should have been their academic priorities.
- I found the value systems espoused by these groups to be based on racial and ethnic prejudice, which were directly contrary to what I thought the substance of a liberal arts culture should be.
- I found many of "the brothers" to be anti-intellectual and dismissive of serious intellectual pursuits.
- Many of them were pursuing majors and occupations I did not respect because they were based on the study of "business," which I regarded as an inferior academic field! I am embarrassed now by that kind of intolerance on my part, and this is not a view I have today.

Yes, I had become indignantly intolerant. And I acted on this. Dan Berman and I booked a large room in the student center and took out ads in the student newspaper in which the two of us challenged the fraternities to a public debate to justify why they should continue to be allowed at our liberal arts college. We were really hostile, and this was a very public challenge. The big day of the "debate" arrived, and Dan and I learned a very important lesson in politics and resistance to change: "stonewalling." Not a single fraternity member showed for the debate. And neither did anyone else. The rest of the campus community had to have thought we were crazy. Conclusion: I needed to find another way to work within the system to change the system. And I would and did in my senior year after Dan graduated and went on to graduate school to leave me alone as a student who loved to stir the pot.

Here is a footnote on my life in opposition to fraternities. About 20 years later, after I had become a full professor at USC, a senior student affairs administrator, Mark Shanley, a friend of mine whom I really respected, came to me and pitched a request for me to become a faculty advisor to a social fraternity. He knew he was facing a potential no, as he was well aware of my disdain for fraternity life. His pitch to me was this particular group wasn't your garden-variety fraternity. By this he meant "no hazing, no secret initiation or password, no White Christian clause." This sounded too good to be true, and he piqued my interest. He went on to explain that this group was being launched as a "colony," meaning not yet a full-fledged chapter of a national fraternity, but sort of like one on probationary status. A small nucleus of founding brothers had been formed, led by none other than an art major. Not too many fraternity presidents in my experience have been art majors. So, I weakened my resistance to the point where I agreed to an initial meeting with this group. And the outcome was that I relented and became their faculty advisor, a role I served in for 16 years.

I even let them eventually initiate me, and so I am a brother of Delta Upsilon (DU). Ironically, there was a chapter of DU at Marietta that I would never have joined as an undergraduate. What this shows at the very least is that since college I have become more tolerant and open to new experiences in higher education. And I now understand why fraternally affiliated males give more money as alums and have higher retention and graduation rates than those without fraternity affiliation.

The moral of this story: I have found I can get a lot more accomplished by working from the inside out rather than standing on the outside being highly critical, in this case of a venerated tradition in American higher education. I have always loved the apocryphal statement attributed to Lyndon Johnson: "I would rather have someone inside the tent pissing out, than someone outside the tent pissing in!" I learned that it is a lot easier to stand outside the tent and hurl criticism than to stand inside the tent and try to constructively change the practices inside the tent.

Learning About Concepts I Could Apply Later

One of my important learning activities in college was attending presentations by visiting experts and scholars. One such visit in my junior year was
to hear the highly regarded scholar of the Holocaust, Hannah Arendt. I went
to her presentation and afterward to a smaller group discussion. I had been
enthralled during her talk, and during the small group conversation I sat
right in front of her, literally at her feet, on the carpeted floor like some
kind of groupie hanging on every word. In the discussion I asked her to
expand on her famous descriptor of the mass killings that she characterized
as "the banality of evil."

I was learning in college about the many varieties of human behavior
that I had never thought about before. This process would continue for me,
especially several years later when I became a psychiatric social worker in the
U.S. Air Force, where I could see many examples of what for me were new
behaviors—but none that I would characterize with the phrase "banality of
evil," except for one, which I will share later in this work. But I did learn of
such behavior during the recent Trump Administration where his officials
ordered the mass separation of refugee parents from their children (and more
recently with the atrocities committed by the Russian military against non-
combatants in the Ukraine). I did not want to imagine that this was my
government doing this to helpless migrants, a practice executed by ordinary
Americans doing as they were ordered. To understand this, I had to have
gone to college to appreciate "the banality of evil."

Ending My Junior Year

For the first 3 years of my college experience, I had committed to a social
restriction in the form of a monogamous romantic relationship. While it was
not the intent of this relationship to deprive me of friendships with women
and the opportunity to spend quality time with them, this was its actual
effect. I don't want to imply that I was forced into this. I had entered this
relationship voluntarily, willingly, and I had learned and benefited from it.
But at the end of my junior year, I decided to end it, which I did. This in turn
set the foundation for me to have a far wider range of social and cocurricular
learning experiences with women in my senior year and helped lay my adult
life foundation for some of the most important work I did, primarily with
women colleagues.

And so my junior year ended, one of truly significant intellectual growth
and achievement in college. That summer of 1964 I did not work in the
Can again, as I had in the two previous summers, and instead returned to

my original love of outdoor landscaping work in Connecticut. One morning that August, I read in *The New York Times* of an "unprovoked" attack by North Vietnamese gunboats on two U.S. Navy destroyers, the *Maddox* and the *Turner Joy*, in the Gulf of Tonkin off North Vietnam. As I read this report, I smelled a rat. Somehow, I just had this sinking sense that this was not all that it was reported to be. A few years later with the release of the so-called "Pentagon Papers," we all learned that the United States had indeed violated North Vietnamese territorial waters and was engaged in a hostile activity, which provoked the North Vietnamese response. But that was later. Then, in August 1964, this event became the pretext for President Johnson's going to Congress and asking and receiving support for what became known as the Gulf of Tonkin Resolution, authorizing him to increase U.S. troop levels in South Vietnam, an action that would kill 58,000 other, mostly young, Americans like me, excluding, of course, several million Vietnamese people. And this Congressional resolution was the literal authorization for my being drafted in 1966 into the U.S. military. Of course, this was not known to me in 1964.

For chapter discussion questions, click the link or scan the QR code to visit Appendix C of the Online Compendium.

https://styluspub.presswarehouse.com/uploads/5e35cd13add3605ede5537f
a2a5159aac11d5b57.pdf

4

THE SENIOR YEAR CAPSTONE EXPERIENCE

Ideally, this is the period in an undergraduate's life when it all comes together. I best stated this in the title of a 1998 book I coauthored entitled, *The Senior Year Experience: Transition, Integration, Reflection, and Closure.* In some ways that does say it all for my senior year experience. But I need to elaborate, for this became the experiential period of my future professional life in my own work on "the senior year experience."

My senior year at Marietta was indeed the culmination of the integration of my curricular, academic learning and my development outside of class in student government leadership. It was also the period when I had to make a decision about next steps after college. I would have been perfectly happy to remain at Marietta forever, where in reality I had become a big frog in a very small puddle, but I headed on to be a tadpole in a huge lake, more like a sea.

The Academic Senior Year

I am sure I had an experience or rather a realization in my senior year that has happened to many other college students: "If I could do this over again, I would do . . ." In my case it was finally being able to take four literature courses, two each from two faculty members whom my student mentor, Dan Berman, had been raving about for 4 years: Professors Harold Dean and Gerald Evans. The result was to make me wish I had declared a major in English! The courses were a two-semester sequence of English literature and two literary period courses, one on transcendental writers of the 19th century and another on the modern novel. Thoreau and Emerson had a tremendous influence on my thinking about individualism and "self-reliance" as in Emerson's essay of that same title. All the steps I had been taking during my

3 previous years in college to make the transition from my parent-influenced state of mind to one of much greater intellectual and personal liberation were captured by Emerson. I felt like I had discovered my spiritual godfather. This work was a perfect intellectual bookend to the reading I had done as punishment for excessive class absenteeism in Speech 101, David Reisman's *The Lonely Crowd*. It was Emerson's essay, however, that provided me a kind of manifesto for using self-reliance as the basis for becoming one of Reisman's "other-directed" people. I felt that essay driving me also in everything I was doing in my cocurricular work at the college.

From Emerson's *Self-Reliance*, 1839

Trust thyself.

Society everywhere is in conspiracy against the manhood of every one of its members. Society is a joint-stock company in which the members agree for the better securing of its bread to each shareholder, to surrender the liberty and culture of the eater. The virtue in most request is conformity. Self-reliance is its aversion. It loves not realities and creators but names and customs.

Whoso would be a man must be a nonconformist.

Let us affront and reprimand the smooth mediocrity and squalid contentment of the times.

Life only avails, not the having lived.

In sum, both in college and in Emerson's encouragement of me to be more intellectually and personally independent, as a senior I had discovered in the college curriculum my lifelong intellectual and mission manifesto!

I need to say this explicitly. I loved being a college student, emphasis on *student*. I loved the reading, thinking, term-paper research, and writing. I also loved talking with professors, visiting them in their offices, and being invited to their homes. By the time I was a senior I had more hours than I needed to graduate, so I could have coasted with an easy five-course load. But, no, there were more courses that I wanted to take, and so I took six per semester, as I had done in my previous junior year, and also 6 more hours that I audited, an 8.00 a.m. Monday/Wednesday/Friday course in Far Eastern history taught by Professor R.L. Jones.

I loved Professor Jones's mind but not the way he graded: multiple-choice tests. Hence, I took the audit route. I also wanted to avoid another painful repeat lesson from him. I had taken 20th-century British history from him the previous year, and he had given me a very challenging intellectual experience. His standard learning device was the use of what he called an "annotated bibliography," a reading of at least 20 books, all directed to addressing one question, in this case: "Was British foreign policy toward Germany the primary cause of World War II?" And this is where I got a little too big for my intellectual britches.

In the required paper I had the nerve to take issue with my professor that there was a fundamental flaw in *his* thinking (not mine) as to a "primary cause." I criticized his assignment as an effort to get us students thinking in a deterministic manner, using one explanatory variable line of reasoning, instead of using multiple causation. He did not appreciate my assessment of his pedagogy and gave me a B on my paper (I still received an A for the course). I marvel in retrospect at precisely what college students remember many years later about these academic demi-gods. In this case, "RL," as the students dubbed him, had a memorable style of teaching. He would stride into the class right as the bell tower clock was chiming the hour. At the last strike of the hour, he would remove a gold pocket watch, open it, and lay it flat on a table. No greetings to the class, nothing. He would pick up exactly where he had left off at the end of the previous class. He never used any notes at all. After exactly 50 minutes, he would retrieve his watch, close it, and walk out of the room. No goodbyes. Not a word. And he never took questions during his lecture. But I still loved the way his mind worked.

My Living Environment: Finally, Outside a "Dorm"

This was a unique year because it was the first of my four that I had not lived in what we used to call "dorms," a now antiquated term that shouldn't be used by practicing academics. It so happened that one of my junior year roommates was a professional bird watcher, a professor's kid (PK), Doug Gill, who aspired to earn a doctorate in ornithology. At some point as a student he had met an elderly local woman on a birdwatch, one Mrs. White. She really became fond of Doug and invited him to live in her home for the coming year while she made a trial move back to Columbus, Ohio, where she had lived previously as the former Ohio governor's wife. Her conditions for Doug's using her home were that he would recruit two other rent-paying young men and that we would promise never to allow women to enter the home. The house would come along with her "maid," and we were to be allowed to use all her china and silver. Naturally, I leapt at the opportunity. It was a grand house and bargain, one block from the campus and across the street from a sorority house.

One weekend night, the third roommate, a normally well-behaved serious student, had fallen off the wagon and returned to the house late along with two inebriated females. One accompanied him into his room. The other came into my room where I had already "retired" for the night. When she woke me and threw herself down on my bed, all I was could think was one thing: I was about to violate my promise to Mrs. White. I leapt out of bed, threw on some clothes, left the house, and spent the night on a residence hall lounge sofa. These are the experiences that truly develop character in college students. My room was to be a sacrosanct place, for studying and sleeping only, and one in which I got the privilege of using the former governor's state office chair. And I loved it.

The sanctity of my room was violated one other time when 2 weeks before my second-semester final exams, someone broke into the home and stole only one thing: all my class lecture notebooks. This had to have been someone who really had it in for me and who knew about my legendary note-taking prowess, the sole secret behind my straight A's. Yes, I had made a lot of enemies by then, as I will relate subsequently. Thus, my senior year transcript reads 10 A's and 2 B's. My roommate, by the way, the birdwatcher, went on to the University of Michigan, earned his PhD in biology, and had a career as a prominent biologist at the University of Maryland. He and I have remained in correspondence.

The Senior Year Cocurricular Experience

I have reflected about the college experience in which I learned the most that now applies to my adult work of being a change agent for the academy. That experience was being a participant in student government as a college senior, what we would now call a "cocurricular" experience!

By the time I had finished my junior year I had become a real thorn in the side of the Greek-dominated student culture of the college. And I was regarded as a "GDI," a god-damned independent. Incidentally, I have not heard that acronym used on any of the more than 500 campuses I have visited in my career post college. But it was used extensively at Marietta College in the 60s. Now I have to hand it to those frat boy student government politicians. They were plenty savvy. And their very clever strategy of silencing me as an outside critic of their system was twofold: Bring me into the system so I could no longer criticize it in the same manner, and give me so much to do to keep me so busy that I wouldn't have time to go after them as I had my junior year. How did they accomplish this? By appointing me as the chief justice of the newly created Student Judicial Council, which had the role of enforcing the student code of academic integrity and investigating and punishing students for infractions of that code (read: cheating and plagiarism).

I brought into this new challenge what was by now a fully developed character trait: tenaciousness. A previous manifestation of this had been evident when I was working in the can factory and had been rightfully accused by the union shop steward of "killing the job." Later in my career at USC, this character trait would be described by one of my two "enemies" on campus, the university librarian. This concept of enemies was brought to my attention during a search application interview when I was being interviewed by the University's chancellor for regional campuses and continuing education in association with the president's wanting me to become the new vice chancellor. The chancellor asked me what I thought was a truly novel question: "John, who are your enemies?" My answer: the university librarian and the director of athletics. How those two had achieved that enemy status (one I was proud of) is another story. But that one enemy, the director of university libraries, used to say about me publicly: "John Gardner has just one problem: He knows only one speed, full-speed ahead!" And he was correct. This is what I meant by "tenaciousness."

Full-speed ahead was my pace in this new role as the founding chief officer of a student-run system of justice enforcing a code of academic integrity. I became a fanatic about rooting out cheating and plagiarism. I really went over the top. It became a messianic crusade. And a primary target of mine was the long-standing practice of Greek organizations maintaining so-called "files" of old tests and exams that were being regularly trotted out by faculty who, for whatever reason, weren't revising their exams, thus giving Greek-letter students a huge unfair advantage versus GDIs like me. Another focus of my work was stamping out plagiarism in English 101 in the regular "theme"-writing regimen. To effect any change in these practices meant I had to work with faculty to try to persuade them to alter their testing practices. And that meant working through the faculty governance system, the curriculum committee, the faculty council, and thus centuries of accumulated tradition and practice. Changing the system had to be addressed then from the inside with the owners, creators, and maintainers of that system—the faculty. System change also came about through enforcement of statutory but previously unenforced codes of conduct. In my 10 months or so as chief justice, I presided over several dozen cases of cheating, plagiarism, and even one office burglary to steal an upcoming examination.

My most significant case, though, was my first. The way the student judicial system worked was that an incident of prohibited practice had to be reported either by a faculty member or a fellow student. This would lead to an investigation and fact gathering. Then, assuming there was sufficient evidence to adjudicate the alleged offense, permission had to be sought by me from the college's president to proceed to a hearing. The hearing was to be conducted at an undisclosed location, date, and time. In my first case a prominent student leader was reported for using plagiarized material in a publicly given speech. I even remember to this day the famous person who had written the purloined material! The speech was a matter of public record, and I found the original unattributed primary source. I met with the president and received my first really hardball lesson on how colleges work. When the president learned the identity of the alleged perpetrator, he was very distressed and told me this could become a major public relations problem for the college. He told me the college was about to embark on a very public fund-raising campaign and how sensitive he was to any potentially adverse publicity. The president was quick though, I have to hand it to him. He immediately offered me a "deal." The deal was this: He would deny my request to prosecute this particular case and individual; and in return he would commit to supporting any and all such future requests I might make that year; and I would execute a confidentiality agreement. Done. I learned at some point the truth of the maxim attributed to President Lyndon Johnson: "Half a loaf is better than no loaf at all!" I took the half loaf and quit while I was ahead, but only on that case.

All of this made me quite notorious, respected by some, reviled by others, but noticed by most on this small campus. The student newspaper even asked me to pose for a photo up in the college's belltower looking out and down on the campus with a spyglass. There I was—a future liberal higher education leader advocating spying on his fellow students. Who would have thought?

Eventually I came to learn a lesson that generations of college leaders have learned and given thanks for: the student leaders, nuisances, troublemakers, are only around for 4 (or 5 or even 6) years, but eventually they move on (unlike your critics in the ranks of the tenured full professors). They have to. It's the only way they get their degrees. And that was to be my fate too.

What was a student like me to do after college? I had excelled academically and in the cocurriculum. I was a promising young leader. I had excellent writing, analytical, and critical reasoning skills. I had learned how to be a change agent within bureaucratic systems. But my government, world affairs, my privileged background (for once), and my good health conspired against me. Why? How? Because this was early 1965, a terrible year for an able-bodied young American male to graduate from college. There was a war going on in southeast Asia that had an insatiable appetite for citizens like me, and it wanted to turn us into citizen soldiers through the "draft." As the Selective Service System operated in 1965, so-called "deferments" from serving on active duty were being granted for these reasons: (a) significant physical health or mental impairment factors, (b) insufficient intelligence as measured by the AFQT (Armed Forces Qualifying Test), (c) being married, (d) enrollment in graduate school, (e) enrollment in seminary or employment as a minister, and (f) employment in national defense industrial occupations. I was in real trouble. I was in good health, of above-average functioning intelligence, single, no interest in becoming a minister or a defense contractor employee. So, what option would I chose to attempt to escape the draft?

What about graduate school? I did not have a major, although I did have lots of academic interests. My friend, Dan Berman, once again rescued me and told me about a graduate field he had discovered: the study of American civilization, that is, American Studies. And what could one do with such a degree? The options were teaching at the college level, conducting research, working in a museum, and so forth.

And what about the marriage option? As I looked around me, many of my classmates in the Class of 65 were opting for marriage driven by the war in Vietnam. I wisely concluded I was not mature enough for marriage, assuming anyone would have had me.

So, over the Christmas break in 1964–1965 I applied to eight graduate schools in American studies. I was admitted to all eight, was offered money from four, and chose the one that offered me the most money: Purdue University. I didn't select Brown, Penn, or Claremont, institutions that offered me more prestige but less money. The money really mattered, because as I have stated previously, my father wouldn't pay for anything he didn't approve of, and he didn't think graduate school was any preparation for what he called "the real world!" Hence he had let me know that I was to be off the dole when I graduated with a bachelor's degree unless I did what he wanted me to pursue: go to law school.

My undergraduate college world ended suddenly, and I hated to leave this environment where I had truly become self-actualized, a model college student in many respects. I marvel now that even though I was an outstanding student, regularly praised and affirmed by my faculty, not a single one of them ever suggested to me, let alone encouraged me, to become a college professor. In those days the economy was roaring. Everyone got jobs after finishing college. It was not assumed that students needed help in finding or even thinking through postcollege employment. There were no "career-planning" services. For that kind of thinking we were left on our own. And the war was roaring too. The outside world was really going to come crashing in on me about 6 months after college, but I didn't know that then. I had to leave college with a diploma to find that out. I am amazed now in retrospect that I received no formal assistance as a senior in developing even an initial plan for life after college. That just wasn't done in those days and times. It was still sink or swim. And I had no helicopter parents to do it for me either.

In conclusion, my undergraduate experience had given me perfect experiential preparation for

- dealing with homesickness
- making a transition from home and differentiating from family norms
- becoming profoundly engaged in both the curriculum and cocurriculum
- developing an adult life while sustaining a system of core values and relationships
- building my character through intercollegiate athletics and cocurricular group membership
- serving my country
- pursuing the cause of the unfinished civil rights movement
- figuring out in my own unique way how I could pursue an adult life in search of justice

I didn't know it then, but I was ready to become an equity warrior within the system because the core intellectual foundation had been laid. This was even though, or perhaps in spite of, the fact that I attended a college where there were

- only two Black students I can remember over 4 years
- few students doing remunerative work on campus while being full-time students
- no part-time and no commuting students—as far as I knew
- no transfer students
- no jock majors and no athletic scholarships
- very few women faculty—only three of my 40 undergraduate courses were taught by women

There was, however, significant student attrition at Marietta. Many students flunked out or dropped out. There was no academic support. No counseling center. No career-planning center. No first-year seminar. Many students, particularly Greek-affiliated males, became young alcoholics.

The academic expectations were high. There were heavy reading and writing loads in most all courses as well as challenging examinations and research requirements. More was demanded of me than I ever demanded of my students at USC. I was a survivor and a college-educated person of privileged origin and social capital. I was headed for graduate school and all kinds of other experiences that I could not then predict. I left college truly grateful to my alma mater and to my father for making the original deal with me to go to college in the first place. In so many, many ways, Marietta College made me whatever it is that I am today. Thank you, Marietta!

What did I do right after college? I went home. I bought a car (a 1960 Karman Ghia) with the $500 dollar graduation gift my father gave me after telling me that was the last money he was ever going to give me and from that point, "Son, you are on your own!" He meant and practiced what he said. Too much gifted money he believed would have spoiled me and compromised my keenly and intentionally developed self-reliance. I went back to work in "the Can" before starting graduate school 3 months later. Believe me, both the summer after college graduation and the whole academic year after graduation were huge let downs. It was for students like me that about 30 years later as a full professor at USC I would develop a course to help departing seniors: University 401—The Senior Year Experience—to better cope with this important transition for life after college.

For chapter discussion questions, click the link or scan the QR code to visit Appendix C of the Online Compendium.

https://styluspub.presswarehouse.com/uploads/5e35cd13add3605ede5537f
a2a5159aac11d5b57.pdf

Interlude

GRADUATE SCHOOL

Even the Military Would Be Better Than This

Compared to my reflections on and analysis of the personal and professional impact of my undergraduate experiences, this section on my graduate school experience is going to be very brief. In retrospect, that is very telling. In truth, my graduate school period was overshadowed by the great event for males of my generation: the Vietnam War. As I started school again that fall, the war was looming over me. It lurked and hungered for me, and I just couldn't get it out of my mind.

I left one unique higher education sector, the small, residential, liberal arts college, and headed for another, the very large, land-grant, research university. Half as many people lived in my "graduate house" residence hall facility at Purdue (about 750) as had attended my alma mater. The day I arrived and checked into my room, I found a female student dressed only in undergarments lying on one of the two beds. Naturally, I was surprised. At Marietta coed visitation was strictly prohibited. Never at a loss for words, I asked her if she came with the room. She replied that she did not and was just waiting for my roommate to return.

I had been awarded the highest prestige fellowship this university awarded. I was a Purdue University Fellow, the award for which included every cent of my tuition and fees and a $200 monthly living stipend for 12 months. My rent was $60 a month, leaving $140. I allowed myself $3.00 a day for meals: $2.00 for dinner and $1.00 split between breakfast and lunch. I was always hungry. After rent and meals, I had $50.00 a month for all other expenses and no money I could count on from my parents, who did not approve of my choice of Purdue or my field.

My roommate, within 2 weeks, found another woman and moved out to live with her. But he didn't want his parents to know about this, so he continued to pay his room rent to maintain his mailing address. Thus,

I lived alone. I had no assistantship duties of any kind because I was a Purdue Fellow. Hence, I did not have a fellow graduate peer group for support. Other than my roommate, whom I rarely saw, I didn't know a soul at this very big university. I had no social life. No dates. I had dinner alone every night with the company of *The New York Times,* which I continued to buy out of my $50 per month of discretionary money. Three of my four courses I found very boring. Teaching and fellow student stimulation was nothing of the caliber I had come to know and expect in undergraduate school. I was not involved in anything other than my academic work. I did have an academic advisor whom I found available but pretentious and not personable enough for me to have a relationship.

What did all this add up to? Straight A's for my first semester. And straight loneliness and acute depression. I was really depressed. I had experienced a great loss of something I truly loved—my undergraduate experience where I had a persona. I was someone. I was known. I was engaged. I had a mission. That was no more.

Sometime early in the winter/spring term a notice arrived from my draft board to report for my induction physical. Ironically, the local demographics of my draft board in Norwalk, Connecticut, did not leave enough unemployed 18–24-year-olds for the draft board to draft and fulfill its quotas. For this country, what was overall a poor man's war had become a war shared by the privileged people like me: able-bodied males with a college degree. This triggered a spate of irrational behavior on my part. I became so disgusted by and alienated in my university life, so lonely, that I dropped out, drove back to Ohio to see a young woman, then drove home and was chastised by my parents. So, I returned to Purdue, more lost than ever.

After a few days back, I left and went home again. After even more humiliation, I returned to Purdue and presented myself to the mental health clinic on a Friday afternoon. I demanded to be "seen" by someone immediately. I was seen by the university's senior psychiatrist, Dr. Wilms. I owe him a great deal. I returned to my classes and then went down to Indianapolis for my Selective Service System physical. I passed with flying colors—first test I had ever truly wanted to fail but didn't have the courage or lack of conscience to fake it. I couldn't persuade myself that I really was a conscientious objector, even though I had extreme reservations about the Vietnam War, its basis, rationale, and legitimacy. I finished that term with four A's and one B—my only B of my master's program. On that one and only assignment for the course, all the professor wrote on my paper was "OK" for what I had concluded was the most original piece of thinking I had done all year. I returned for summer school and 9 more hours of A's. By then I had applied for officer training in the U.S. Air Force as a strategy for avoiding the infantry and beating the odds. My eyesight limitations prevented me from being a "rated" (flying status) officer, so the Air Force had to find something else for me to do. Ultimately, they did. I finished my master's in August of 1966, 36 whopping hours in 12 months, and was inducted into the Air Force on October 16, 1966. There isn't much more to be said about this relatively brief period as a graduate student other than I left Purdue feeling like damaged goods and having no idea what a striking contrast lay immediately ahead of me in the Air Force, one that would prepare me to be an effective college educator and a truly *woke* citizen when it came to matters of race, class, and opportunity that subsequently intersected in the collegiate environment.

By the way, as I have aged my sentiments about the value of my Purdue experience have mellowed and matured, and I was awarded an honorary doctoral degree by Purdue in 2000. I also hold an honorary degree from Purdue's archrival, Indiana University.

Now on to the transformative military experience.

PART TWO

MY LIFE AND LEARNINGS IN THE U.S. AIR FORCE

5

I SHOULD HAVE PAID
THE AIR FORCE

When I look at the formative experiences of my life that prepared me to be a champion for greater equity in higher education, there was no greater experience for showing me what equity could look like than my 2 years on active duty with the U.S. Air Force. The Air Force, a unique society of its own, was, in many respects, unlike the society in which I had spent my previous 22 years. What an unexpected context in which to have this realization given how I had acquired in college and graduate school a fair number of biases and prejudices about what "the military" was really like. And, like most prejudices, I came to learn that many of mine were totally unfair and unfounded. In a sentence, what I experienced in the Air Force was an "equity laboratory" unlike anything I could have found under the auspices of the United States at that time. Thank you, U.S. Air Force! I also have to thank the Air Force for "ordering" me to become a college teacher and for giving me an extraordinary educational opportunity that has made me a much more effective professor, manager, and leader—namely as a psychiatric social worker.

To remind you, up to this point in my 22 years I was a product of lily-White U.S. society; there were almost no children of color in my entire U.S. school history including college. It didn't take me long to realize that the U.S. Air Force was going to be a very different society for me, one in which I would not only see considerable numbers of persons of color, but also in leadership roles to whom I would be responsible.

My Introduction to Military Life

I had signed on for a 2-year commitment to officer training in the Air Force and then active duty—2 years active and 4-years active reserve. In basic training I had my first Black "teacher" in my life, and wow, he was/ is memorable. I refer to a man I only knew as "Sergeant Small," my drill sergeant. Prior to his coming to his duty station at Lackland Air Force Base, he had been one of President Lyndon Johnson's White House Honor Guards. To say that was one proud man doesn't do him justice. I had never met anyone so proud of what he was doing and who he was. He was on a mission. He just exuded pride; he commanded and received my respect. He was the first, and not the last in the Air Force to tell me what I had to do. I estimate he had to have been at least 6 feet, 8 or 9 inches tall. I don't think I had ever been in proximity to such a tall person and one of such force of energy and personality.

The first thing he taught me was that the very best teachers are those who demonstrate pride in their purposes for being a teacher. I have attempted to practice this over my whole career, inspired by him, but surely not equaling him in this respect. He was also a master of pedagogy. Here are two examples that influence me to this day as a public communicator and teacher. He would shout at us: "First, I am going to tell you what I am going to learn you. Then I am going to learn you. Then I am going to tell you what I learned you!" And he would keep doing that until we *all* achieved mastery. There was no drill-instructor grading on the curve.

Besides this important lesson in instructional pedagogy, another important lesson I learned from Sergeant Small, the value of which I didn't realize until about 8 years later when I was directing the University 101 program at USC. It had to do with my learning how to orient new students to the university so that they would survive and thrive—just like Sergeant Small was trying to do for us in basic training. His teaching was really about what we now call "sense of belonging" and it went like this:

Do you want to survive Vietnam? (Response expected: "*Yessir!*")

Then listen up.

There is a right way . . .

And there is a wrong way . . .

And there is the Air Force Way.

And I am going to learn you the Air Force Way!

Thanks to Sergeant Small I would actually tell my students in University 101, "There is a right way, wrong way, and the USC way, and if you want to survive and do well here you must learn the university way, and that's exactly what we are going to teach you." To be even more explicit, what we were doing intentionally was to teach first-year students to *love* the university and being a student there. And over 50 years we have come to learn through our assessment that this effort accounts more than anything else for the powerful sense of belonging that first-year students develop in and through this course. I now know that one of the biggest problems we face in improving college student retention is creating in them this all-important sense of belonging.

But aside from my beneficial exposure to the instructional prowess of Sergeant Small, my nearly 3 months in officer and basic training were an unwelcome shock to my system. I had literally gone from being a high-performing graduate student on a university campus to a totally different environment, one where individual differences, critical thinking, and independent thinking and acting were not prized, at least in the training stages. And I was miserable. The only good day I had in 3 months was the one day I was allowed off base, Christmas Eve, when we were bused to downtown San Antonio. We were dropped off in front of the Alamo where a sign greeted us "Welcome to the Alamo, Open Every Day of the Year Except December 24," so I missed it. We were greeted as we disembarked from the bus literally by a line of prostitutes, offering their services, as they do in every military training town in the world.

My father, though, had given me advice as to how to spend that one day, advice that for once I took: dinner at a fine restaurant that he chose for me; a visit to the world-famous San Antonio Zoo; and a shopping excursion to a business that claimed it was "the world's largest second-hand book store"—Brock's—7 million volumes to choose from, several of which I bought to smuggle back in to my base quarters where books of any kind were strictly forbidden. That stricture was another huge adjustment for me. One life change I made of relatively little consequence was the one night I was allowed in the officers' club on base. I had my first cocktail ever at age 22, a whisky sour. The Air Force had driven me to do something I had sworn I would never do as an adult child of an alcoholic. Thankfully, this never became a problem for me. The experience was definitely one of exposure for me to a wider swath of American society than I had ever interacted with before.

After finishing 3 months of training in San Antonio, I had an opportunity to request a change of "military occupational specialty" from one that I was told was a plum assignment, an investigator in the "Office of Special Investigations," charged with investigating the most serious crimes, including espionage, to one that I thought of as more benevolent and humane: becoming a psychiatric social worker. To my astonishment, the Air Force not only considered my wishes in this matter but reassigned me.

It was explained to me that in this year, 1966, the service was ramping up its medical corps significantly due to the Vietnam conflict and was trying, in particular, to expand its psychiatric services. As I later learned, this was to reduce the dependency of the Air Force on the U.S. Army for psychiatric services, a field of military medicine in which the Army had been the leader since World War II. It was also explained to me that when the Army Air Corps was split off from the Army in the late 1940s to form the new U.S. Air Force, the commander of this new force (General Curtis LeMay) believed in the superiority of his personnel who were leaving the Army behind. This belief system included the notion that such elite personnel were much less likely to need psychiatric services.

Whatever the background, at the time I was attempting to change my assignment the Air Force was desperate for personnel to serve as social workers in Air Force hospitals and their mental health clinics. This meant specifically that I did not have to have a graduate degree in social work. Another graduate degree would be suitable as long as my preparation included work in the behavioral sciences (which mine did—hours in undergraduate and graduate courses in sociology, especially and psychology, including a course in abnormal psychology), and demonstrated ability in interviewing and writing. The latter two I had acquired extensively in both undergraduate and graduate school. Therefore, with the stroke of a pen I was reassigned as a brand-new psychiatric social worker and sent to a "casual" company to await my orders shipping me to a place called Sumter, South Carolina.

My New Air Force Home and School for Life: Shaw Air Force Base

I hadn't thought of Sumter, South Carolina, for years, but when I arrived, I immediately recalled it as the location of a racist homily from my father about why some people didn't want to work. I was 13 years old and we were on a family drive south from Canada to Florida. Our car had developed engine trouble, and we spent a large part of a day in Sumter while the car was undergoing repairs. I noticed on all the streets I could see a significant number of Black males sitting or standing around, obviously idling. I asked my father why these people weren't working and what were they doing or waiting for. In my Connecticut hometown, the only men I saw were almost always working at something. What I received was a racist explanation about how "these people did not want to work and just wanted to hang out." I learned, exactly 10 years later when I arrived in Sumter, that things hadn't changed much at all—that is, *off* the base. On base, well, it was another world, thanks to the U.S. government as the principal provider of economic opportunity and upward social mobility.

Shaw Air Force Base (AFB), named for a famous WWI pilot and Sumter native, Erwin David Shaw, had been a major installation of the U.S. Army Air Corps dating to 1941, and then the U.S. Air Force. When I was stationed there in the mid-1960s, it was the major training base for all personnel in support of the reconnaissance mission of the Air Force in Vietnam. Basically, Shaw trained all the pilots and all the support crews to accomplish the reconnaissance mission in southeast Asia. While I might have wished I was not a cog in the war machine of a war I was personally opposed to, I was definitely such a cog. The base had approximately 8,000 troops and almost 20,000 military dependents, and I was assigned to the 363rd Tactical Hospital's psychiatric clinic. The "clinic" consisted of two of us, a psychiatrist and me, his social worker. We were the clinic, at least initially. But by the time I finished my tour our staffing had been doubled to four to service almost 30,000 people.

Another way I could describe my new home and reference group, the Shaw AFB 363rd 100-bed tactical field hospital, was that it was a "MASH" unit, just like the fictional one in the celebrated, long-running TV comedy. "MASH" stood for "medical and surgical hospital," and inherent in the concept was that this particular type of military hospital was designed to be "mobile" and "portable." In other words, it could be transformed, picked up, loaded on the C-47's, and flown anywhere in the world. Most all the military personnel stationed in this unit were on what the Air Force called worldwide mobility (WWM) status, which basically meant that (a) in our place of duty at all times we had to keep packed a WWM bag of basic clothing and toilet articles; (b) we had to be ready to leave everything we owned and be on the flight line ready to be boarded within 30 minutes, without even notifying anybody; (c) we had to have an up-to-date "shot record" showing that we were inoculated against any disease we could contract anywhere in the world; (d) we had to have a will; and (e) we had to be qualified on the M-16. After I developed a minimum proficiency in the use of this weapon, I could never understand why my country would allow me, if I so desired, to have one of these for home use!

In terms of the equity laboratory I was about to experience, it's important to remember that this was 1967, just 3 years after the adoption of the Civil Rights Act. On the base *everything* was racially integrated—schools for children, restaurants, movie theater, golf course, hospital, all military facilities, and all housing. *Off* the base was the exact opposite. Going out "the back gate" was like entering another country. Everything was segregated. I went out once just outside the back gate on an ambulance run to recover a hit-and-run civilian casualty. We found him deceased, and so we had to notify the county coroner, who was to come out to claim the body. When the coroner's minions arrived and discovered that the deceased was a Black man, they refused to put him in the ambulance and instead radioed back to have a pick-up truck sent out for livery. In that era, racial prejudice extended well beyond the living to the dead.

Of course, when I arrived at Shaw, fairly late on the evening of January 10, 1967, my intent was to do my tour and then leave South Carolina and get back to my life as a "northerner." How little I knew about how I was about to be transformed. I did not know a soul in South Carolina. I had no connections, no network of any kind, no friend nor family member to turn to.

As I was escorted to my quarters I was told, "Relax, we don't wear hats, or salute, or shine our shoes in the hospital area!" Now that sounded like heaven, the total opposite of the training base I had just come from. The part about the shoes, though, didn't work out that way. My supervisor, the base psychiatrist, told me I needed to keep my shoes so "spit-shined" that "your patients can see their reflection in your shoes." He judged that I needed to offset my very youthful appearance by exhibiting to my patients my respect for military discipline, bearing, and customs.

The next day, January 11, 1967, no doubt was one of the single most important days of my life. As a new troop I was to commence my day with a customary audience with "the commander." I was ushered into his office where he braced me at attention and did not order me "at ease." I looked down at him and saw to my significant surprise that for the first time in my life the most important person in my environment was going to be a Black man. That was my first real hint that I was in for an eye-opening experience and that America finally was changing.

He had my record open and spread out on his desk, and the first thing he did was to take note of my educational level: "Gardner, I see that you have two degrees; that means you are the most educated man in my squadron aside from the physicians!"

I really didn't know what to say other than the all-purpose, tried-and-true response: "Yessir."

He replied, "Gardner, that means you are going to perform 'community service.'"

"Yes sir, but what does 'community service' mean, sir?"

"Gardner, it means whatever I and the Air Force say it means! And in your case, it means you are going to do some college teaching at night when you are officially off duty. We have an extension of USC on base, and I am sure we can get you approved to do some teaching for us."

Still not quite understanding that I really didn't have any options, I said something like, "But, sir, I am not a college teacher. I have never taught anything."

The commander replied, "Gardner, the Air Force needs you to do some college teaching. This is 1967, only 3 years after the Civil Rights Act, and we are desperate down here for qualified teachers. And you will do as I order!"

What could I say other than "Yessir"?

That is how I became a college teacher, only as a result of a direct order from my commander. He immediately ordered me to report to the Base Education Office to talk to USC on-base director, who proceeded to set me up with interviews on the main campus, some 42 miles away, 2 days later on Saturday, January 13, 1967. That was so long ago that there were "Saturday classes"—unknown today by traditional-aged students. I had three interviews and was approved to teach six courses: five history courses and Sociology 101. The history chair who interviewed me, actually in his residence, was a descendent of the Ochs family, the founders of *The New York Times*. His apartment was one grand art museum, revealing the art collector that he was and patron of the local arts scene. In one 42-mile drive I had gone from the world of the U.S. military to a true university environment, and I was going to attempt to somehow live in both simultaneously.

On Becoming a Psychiatric Social Worker

On my first day on duty, I met my other "significant other" in the Air Force, my supervisor, the base psychiatrist, Dr. James Reardon. He was truly surprised to see me and delighted because my absence had meant he was having to do a lot of the grunt work that he was happy to give up. He was aware that the Air Force was sending him "a person" to finally give him some support after he had been on station about 18 months. He immediately set me at ease, addressed me by my first name, a rarity in the military, and invited me to also address him in like manner. Without wasting a moment, he immediately practiced what I was already learning about how the Air Force onboarded new personnel—by two means: first, by giving people extraordinary responsibility and doing so immediately, and second, providing a learning environment where people learn by doing—again, immediately.

He explained to me that my initial most important duty would be to take a "social history" from each new patient—seven to eight a day, and that I would start doing so that very day. "Come on John, what are we waiting for? You get the next patient that I was going to see and do the intake on!" And after he gave me the following primer, off I went to do my first intake interview.

I was instructed to memorize a protocol and never refer to it in writing. I was to work through the protocol of topics/questions, listen thoughtfully, and commit to memory as much as possible of what I was hearing without taking any notes. He explained to me that note-taking might inhibit more honest sharing. I was also instructed not to use the word *why* to pose a question to avoid sounding like I was making a judgment. At the conclusion of the conversation, I was to walk the patient to an appointment clerk for follow-up appointment scheduling, return to my own private office and take down as many notes as I could dash off, which would comprise my outline for my subsequent writing that night of the actual social history. Specifically, I was given the following categories around which to collect and then write the history:

- geographic origin before coming on active duty
- reason(s) for joining the Air Force
- family history
- school history
- health history
- sexual history
- employment history
- Air Force history
- presenting problem
- mental status review
- provisional diagnosis for review and approval/modification by the psychiatrist
- recommendations for follow-up and treatment and/or administrative action(s)

This is what I went to college to learn how to do: listen and write, evaluate, provide feedback, show empathy, make recommendations. With writing seven to eight case histories a day, I wrote more on a daily basis in the Air Force than I ever did in college. I would never have thought that possible.

Besides learning the art and skill of taking and writing a social history, my initial training consisted of something important but of much lower required skill and educational level: learning how to type. That's right, I was 22 with two college degrees and had never learned to type. For the previous 5 years I had been paying people to type all my papers. That would definitely not work in the Air Force. Therefore, I was dispatched to the base typing class where the expectations were these: You will learn to type 35 words per minute with net five errors over the next 6 weeks, 5 days a week, 1 hour a day. At the end of the 6 weeks, I was clocking out at 55 words a minute and feeling quite liberated at having learned to do this.

Part of my role as a social worker also meant leaving the hospital and "going down on base" into the actual units where my patients worked so I could talk to their coworkers, supervisor, or chaplain perhaps. This was necessary to gather insight into the patient's Air Force duty environment in case it became apparent that we needed to make recommendations for any changes in duty.

Also, once I learned what I was doing, I was allowed to do follow-up therapy sessions and lead a weekly therapy group of the younger enlisted men and/or a group of older career, noncommissioned officers. In my work, particularly with the newer and younger troops, I gained wonderful insights into how effective organizations did or did not accomplish effective "orientation" of new arrivals. It would still be my conclusion that the Air Force did a much better job of what we now call "onboarding" of new members to the culture than we do in higher education. As I will relate in chapters 8 and 9, later in my career I was inspired to try to make my own contributions to helping higher education improve its "orientation" of new students. But my foundational thinking for this work was the combination of my own college orientation combined with how I saw the Air Force accomplish orientation much more effectively. In the Air Force I saw very clearly that people could actually be taught how to adapt to new life circumstances and that a body of knowledge and skills was needed and could be taught.

My supervision from Dr. Reardon was initially very close, very personal, very immediate, with constant feedback on what I was observing and reporting about my patients. Reardon's supervision and feedback were also very intense and a constant source of learning and suggestions for improvement. One of the many ways he coached me was to pay attention to how I arranged the furniture in my office. How furniture is placed makes a symbolic statement about differential levels of power and is or is not an encourager or inhibitor of communication. These were subjects I had never considered. Put quite simply, I was never to put the patient on the opposite side of my desk. For the next 50 years of arranging my higher education workspaces, I always practiced what I had learned in this context in the Air Force, and I could see how it definitely influenced patterns of communication and rapport. That was a bottom-line take-away lesson I learned: how to establish rapport with people who were not like me and did not come from affluent backgrounds, as was the case with most all of my Air Force patients.

Some of the patients introduced me to behavioral patterns I would ultimately see in college students and try to help them modify. Many of our patients were unhappy because of their adjustment challenges in the military and were hopeful we could find a psychiatric illness as a basis for a recommendation for medical discharge. These were people who just "wanted out." There also was a cohort of patients who were in disciplinary actions. A supervisor or Air Force attorney would have ordered a psychiatric evaluation to see if there were any medical mitigating factors that could be addressed pretrial. And there were many troops who were having significant relationship issues, especially young, relatively newly married individuals, who found it difficult to manage a marriage, children, and Air Force responsibilities, exacerbated by remote duty tours to southeast Asia. We had many patients who had developed significant alcohol-use problems. Social and habitual drinking was endemic and very, very, affordable due to discounted prices for alcoholic beverages. I can remember clubs on base offering a beer for 15 cents and mixed drinks for a quarter.

The Air Force culture also introduced me to something I had never encountered in college, graduate school, or my home life; namely, adultery. It was endemic. When this was discovered by either party in the relationship, it became a profound source of conflict inviting requests for mediation. The Vietnam War lent itself naturally to this behavioral pattern. This is because most of our troops were stationed with us for training before being shipped to Vietnam, most commonly for a 12-month tour. Before being shipped, the young married couple would be living together, but while they were separated, frequently one or both would be unfaithful. When the husband came home from war, there was hell to pay. I had one patient, a senior noncommissioned officer (NCO) who was an aide to a general in Vietnam, and part of the NCO's duties was procuring women to entertain the general. Unfortunately, the NCO took some photographs of such work and left a few of them in what was called his "field jacket." After the NCO returned to Shaw, his wife found these photos when she took the jacket to the cleaners. The result was that she threatened to kill him, and the NCO came in to see us fearing for his life.

Another common scenario is the new marriage in which the female is very dependent on the male husband who calls all the shots. After he goes away for a year, leaving her behind, and she has to grow up and make her own choices. He comes home and finds not the same woman he left behind but one who is much more independent and not always willing to do anything he might demand. She had changed. He hadn't changed. An explosion erupts and in they come to the psychiatric clinic to get help on the marriage.

Some of our patients just wanted "talk therapy," a legitimate need for sure. They needed help on reflecting on where their lives were leading them and especially for the trauma they had experienced. Many came back from Vietnam profoundly changed by what they had seen and experienced and from drug use. Our patients would leave for Vietnam largely drug free but return a year later with serious drug-use problems. Most of them, as their medical charts revealed, were also being treated for venereal disease. We also had many patients with high-functioning anxiety and/or depression levels. This was understandable as they were headed for an unknown future in a war zone. Many troops were experiencing a profound sense of loss of their former lives, and it was very hard to put Humpty-Dumpty together again. I would learn after my Air Force tour the parallels between what I was seeing in the military environment and the life situations my college students would present to me.

Understandably, the person who was most instrumental in whatever skills I acquired from my Air Force learning experience was my boss, Dr. Reardon (Jim). Here are some of the things he taught me, including those I still mentally practice to this very day

Dr. James Reardon's Eight Principles

I am going to call this "Dr. James Reardon's Eight Principles for the Practice of Military Psychiatry During Wartime." These are the major themes he stressed to make me a decent Air Force therapist. These are also principles for good mental health in any context and success in life, and I have applied these for the rest of my life working in higher education.

- *Adults clean up their own mess!* In my interviewing and compiling social histories, one thing Jim wanted me to be alert to was the patient's potential for better mental health. Was there evidence in patients' lives that they had experienced problems because of personal actions or decisions that they then took control of to resolve? In contrast, which patients presented past problems that always had to be resolved by others and not the patients, if they could be resolved at all? These patients were taking a passive approach. I would listen for reports of such experiences and dutifully record them. I would also try to lead the patient in discussion of the current situation to see if there was anything to be learned from how a former mess was resolved—or exacerbated by the patient's own actions.

- *Does the individual learn from experience?* Look for the patterns. This sounds so simple, but it isn't. Are the circumstances being presented now just one more in a long chain of similar events that have been problematic? Frequently, our patients would present not a new problem at all in the sense of its being created since joining the Air Force, but rather just a repetition of exactly the same kinds of jams the patient had experienced in civilian life. Again, my job was to note and document those patterns and to ask my patient to reflect on them. Does the individual's history show any capacity to learn from experience? Of course, this was another definition of the presence or absence of maturity.

- *Taking responsibility is a sign of maturity and mental health.* "What, who me? I didn't do that. I am not responsible!" The basic question is, when things don't go well, whom do the patients hold responsible—themselves or others? This pattern reveals a great deal of blaming others for personal misfortunes. At extreme levels it may reveal the lack of a conscience and capacity for guilt or remorse. This is especially true of sociopathic personalities who always rationalize their lack of responsibility, show no remorse, and blame and castigate others.

- *"The last base was absolutely the best. This base sucks. The next base will be better!"* I lost track of how often I heard this one. This is the person who always believes that problems will be resolved in some future time and location(base), but definitely not here and now. Again, this is another pattern that, if it is ever to be altered in therapy, required the patient to realize, own, and take some action to alter. In working with such individuals, I had to force them to focus on their present dynamics as opposed to focusing on the past or their future: "We are not here to focus on your childhood. We are here to focus on your present situation and see what we can do to help you address this."

- *Nobody makes you feel anything!* I tried to help patients decide how they interpreted the behaviors of others and how those behaviors were related to them in some way. My message was this: Short of others giving you a direct order in the military, they are not responsible for what you do and feel. They make their own choices, just as you must. And you must do so by emphasizing rational thinking about the realities of what's going on around you. You have to work on your own self talk about how you interpret the ways others are relating to you and how you feel about them. (This approach is what became known in the 60s as rational emotive therapy, a form of cognitive behavioral therapy popularized by Albert Ellis and practiced by my Air Force boss.)

- *Who's in charge here anyway?* I also stressed with patients that while the Air Force can and does control troops in some important ways, like shipping them to Vietnam, patients needed to recognize the areas of their life and patterns of their interactions with others that they control by their choices/decisions, not those of the Air Force. This was self-management 101. In more theoretical language, it was about focusing therapy on the concept of "locus of control."

- *Do individuals have a capacity for laughing at personal foibles and not taking themselves so seriously?* Are they showing any ability to be amused by some of their own behaviors? I was taught to look for such as evidence of patients beginning to emerge from the darkness of depression. Not taking oneself too seriously is a marker of good mental health.

- *"The screwing you get isn't worth the screwing you get!"* Let me contextualize this. I was learning this in the mid-1960s when the Air Force, as a society, was much more open about sexual behavior than the external civilian society from which many of our troops had so recently come. Personnel were given sex-related lectures in basic training unlike the public schools they had been in before entering the military. Off the base, sexual aids, products, especially contraceptive devices were kept well out of sight (ostensibly to protect children), and one had to request such from the pharmacist. Not in the military. Condoms were right out there on display at checkout along with candy and cigarettes and the *National Enquirer*. The reality was that sex was everywhere in the military! And that meant that many of our patients were relatively very young and sexually active and had made a lot of bad choices around their sexual behaviors, often in a serial fashion, with one individual after another, hence demonstrating that they did not learn from experience. And what they could have learned from experience was that the sex they had engaged in turned out not to be worth the inherent dangers. Our job was to help our patients think this through. While I never kept a count, I think I heard my boss quote this mantra in our regular review of our patients' situations more than anything else he would recite: "The screwing you get isn't worth the screwing you get." Literally, with the troops I evaluated after returning from Vietnam, I almost never saw a medical record that did not reveal treatment for venereal disease while in and post-Vietnam. No fun.

Of course, I couldn't have known it at the time, namely while I was on active duty and before becoming a full-time higher education professional, but so many of these behavioral patterns would apply to my future college students and some of their faculty and staff too. Thank you, Dr. Jim Reardon and the U.S. Air Force!

Winning the Mentor Lottery Again

After being supervised by my first psychiatrist for about 8 months, Reardon finished his 2-year tour and moved back to his native California. For a month or so I was the clinic of one as I waited for his replacement to arrive. I continued to do my intake interviews and histories, calling upon other physicians for matters that needed immediate diagnosis and medical attention. Eventually, a new psychiatrist arrived, Dr. William King, who couldn't have been more different from Dr. Reardon. This provided another great learning experience for me, coupled with even more responsibility. Unlike Jim Reardon, who was a practitioner of new trends in psychiatric treatments and a very practical, "let's do whatever we can to get the troop functioning," Bill King was a very traditional, classically trained Freudian psychoanalytic therapist. He was a practicing Catholic (a rarity in the profession, I learned) who had entered the Air Force straight from doing his psychiatric residency at a highly specialized Catholic hospital, the Seton Institute, in Baltimore. I was to learn many years later that it was this same hospital to which Catholic clergy who were caught up in the Boston pedophilia scandal were dispatched. Here, Dr. King had had all kinds of time and opportunity to do intensive psychoanalytic therapy with very bright patients well equipped to profit from such, namely priests and nuns. Those kinds of patients were extraordinarily different from our patients in the military, many of whom did not have the verbal or intelligence levels to profit from traditional psychoanalytic therapy. More importantly, because of our patient load there was no way Dr. King was going to be able to see all of our patients three times a week, let alone daily, for talk therapy.

This was a significant adjustment for him and soon we made a pact. He realized he needed me to teach him how the Air Force really functioned, and in return he knew there was a great deal he could—and did—teach me. While he was definitely my supervisor, who was far better trained than I and who outranked me, my superior knowledge of how the Air Force worked and how to work the system to get things done for our patients was really helpful to him and somewhat narrowed our natural hierarchical differences. Dr. King remained my supervisor for the next 14 months or so until I finished my tour, and he and I remained in touch until his death about 10 years ago. With both these physicians I really won the mentor lottery.

Summing Up: Why All This Mattered

To understate the reality, there was great need for the services we were providing. The work was far more rewarding than I could have hoped to have for a duty assignment. On some days I thought it was I who should be paying the Air Force for all that I was learning. Truly, the work was fascinating, challenging, and meaningful. Yes, I was learning a tremendous amount, but I also could reasonably conclude from the feedback I was receiving from my patients that I was helping them help themselves.

It can be reasonably asked—and is being asked by some thoughtful educators—how can privileged White people, especially older White men, possibly have the kinds of experiences and background that would provide them with sufficient understanding, empathy, compassion, let alone commitment to be effective in today's efforts to increase the equity levels of opportunities and outcomes for less advantaged college students. Of course, I can speak primarily to my own life experiences such as my intellectual preparation in college and graduate school; my summer work as a steelworker; my active-duty time in the Air Force; and my 5 years' teaching in a federally funded antipoverty educational program, about which I will write later—TRIO Upward Bound; and then my 32 years as a university professor for thousands of first-generation, Pell-eligible students in South Carolina. I can also argue more broadly that to win requisite support for these deserving students *all* of us have to be aboard. In my own case I am well persuaded that the sum total of my experiences prepared me as well as any man of privilege could ever be prepared to make significant contributions to the cause of advancing equity. And it is to the Air Force that I assign much of this experiential credit. Thank you, U.S. Air Force!

It was in the Air Force that I lived, ate, slept, and worked with all types of fellow citizens from across our country but primarily from lower socioeconomic groups who were experiencing in many ways a higher standing of living than they had in their civilian lives. In the military there was no food or shelter insecurity. And everyone had free medical care and clothing. All could enroll in college-credit courses with Uncle Sam picking up 75% of the tab. The Air Force was a step up in lifestyle, especially for those from the poorest region of the United States, the Southeast. No wonder a disproportionate proportion of the career-enlisted and officer corps came from there. In my period of service, women were dramatically underrepresented. The only women who served with me were nurses in our hospital. Hispanics were also underrepresented. But Blacks were overrepresented. And nothing about the Air Force could have been more different from my home of origin. Thank goodness.

While I can easily enumerate all the influences of my military experience that have made me effective as a college educator improving opportunities and outcomes for less advantaged students, I think the most important impact of the military experience was on my realization of the importance of living the mission.

It's All About Mission

I had entered the Air Force at age 22, with two degrees, undergraduate and graduate, never having been introduced to the concept of mission. Now it is second nature to me. It is who I am. No one had ever asked me to even think about the merits of having a mission, of being mission driven. But immediately upon entering the Air Force I was introduced to the concept of mission. It was mission that united us all. It was mission that we all had in common no matter what differences we exhibited in our previous civilian lives. We all were to live—and some of us to die—for the mission. The mission was more important than any single one of us. The overall mission trumped any individual thing of importance to any one of us. Believe me, we all knew the mission.

To be specific, we had to first learn the mission of the Air Force. Then we moved on to learn the mission of the major subunits of the Air Force known as "commands." I was a member of the Tactical Air Command (TAC), the mission of which was to provide direct combat air support for U.S. Armed Forces and our allies. Then within TAC there were individual bases, each with a distinct mission. I had to understand my base's mission: to manage all the reconnaissance aspects of the war in southeast Asia, and, in particular, to take the photographs necessary for plotting bombing and other missions to wage war against the enemy and to protect our troops. Within our base we were divided into "squadrons," each one with unique missions all in support of the base mission to support the command mission to support the Air Force mission.

In particular I was to serve the 363rd Tactical Hospital mission to provide health-care support for 8,000 troops and 19,000 dependents. And within the hospital squadron and its mission, I had to pursue, every day, the mission of my unit in the hospital, the psychiatric clinic. While on a personal basis I was strongly opposed to the war in Vietnam, which made me a tiny cog in our overall war machine, I was strongly in favor of doing everything I could to accomplish our mission of providing the best possible mental health care. For the first time in my life, I had a mission. And I loved it. I thrived on it as I had never thrived before. That was a lesson for me. The Air Force like no other organization in my experience had given me opportunity, responsibility, and training to pursue this mission. I would continue pursuing some similar elements of mission for the rest of my life. I saw this immediately applicable when I joined the faculty and eventually the senior administration of USC. We had a mission to serve the people of South Carolina. In particular, my mission was to serve those students who were most vulnerable to not surviving: first-year students, especially those who were not from privileged backgrounds. And since "early retirement" from the university in 1999, I have had the opportunity to pursue a related but new mission in my role as cofounder and CEO of a nonprofit organization dedicated to continuing the unfinished civil rights movement by improving undergraduate student success, especially for those students who have historically received the least equitable treatment.

For chapter discussion questions, click the link or scan the QR code to visit Appendix C of the Online Compendium.

https://styluspub.presswarehouse.com/uploads/5e35cd13add3605ede5537f
a2a5159aac11d5b57.pdf

6

BECOMING AN INVOLUNTARY COLLEGE EDUCATOR AND DISCOVERING MY CALLING

For my entire period of active duty, I was on a parallel journey of preparation for becoming a future higher education leader and equity advocate and champion. As I have reported, it was the Air Force and my hugely influential Black commander who had ordered me to become a college teacher. Thus, my initial college teaching experiences took place in a very formative period of almost 2 years while I was on active duty. Again, had the Air Force not enabled and required me to teach, I speculate that I would not be here today in my current occupational status.

My First Campus: USC at Lancaster

On January 13, 1967, I was approved to teach six courses for USC's Extension Division. The university wanted me to start right away, as in 2 weeks, teaching an Introduction to Sociology course at the campus in Lancaster, a classic South Carolina mill town where a major national textile firm (Springs) had two large mills. It was a true company town in that all life revolved around the mill(s).

Opened originally in 1959, the USC campus had grown enough by 1965 to move from its original downtown location to a brand-new building on the outskirts of town. Enrollment was about 500, still all White when I arrived, and nonresidential. Associate in Science and Arts degrees were offered to encourage students to transfer to the flagship campus in Columbia, to finish a bachelor's degree. The students were almost all first generation and

"Pell eligible," and most of them were either the children of mill workers or mill workers themselves. There were then huge differences in backgrounds between me and my students, which gave me another wonderful opportunity for both learning and service to others, all while I was on active duty in the Air Force.

Apparently, I was the only adjunct the university could find to teach this course that semester, and because I was on duty in the Air Force Mondays through Fridays from 7:30–4:30, I could not teach at a conventional time. The university agreed to schedule the class at the only time that would work for me: Friday evenings from 7:30 to 10:00 p.m. I was initially very reluctant to start teaching my first college course without more time, at least a few months, to prepare. But the university vice president who offered me the position told me in all seriousness that such preparation time was not really necessary and that "John, anything that comes out of your mouth will educate these students!" He was not, in reality, being condescending or dismissive of the quality of these students. He really meant what he said, which was both his commentary on what he perceived my potential to be and on what he knew to be the level of preparation of the students I was about to encounter.

My First Teaching Experience in Rural South Carolina

I really was nervous about beginning to teach. Thus far, my only formal preparation in public speaking was my Speech 101 course that I had taken 6 years before and received a grade of D. I had done no teaching in graduate school, as my fellowship did not carry any teaching responsibilities. Literally then, I had never taught anything in my life. But like many adjuncts, that wasn't going to stop me. Just a few days short of my 23rd birthday I taught my first class, manifesting some symptoms of what my psychiatrist boss, Jim Reardon, flippantly, although correctly, labeled as "adult situational anxiety reaction." I was definitely anxious. I knew the symptoms to expect: nervousness, significant appetite loss, and mild headache. I made the 65 or so–mile drive from my base north to Lancaster, skipped dinner, which I was not sure I could keep down, and passed restaurants that on later trips I would observe had posted signs: "We Reserve the Right NOT to Serve Anyone"—referencing people for whom I was an advocate. I was very concerned about my appearance as I was just a month out of Air Force training. I had very little hair and was concerned I would look younger than many of my students. And I did. But to make myself look older than I was and to communicate some kind of authority, I wore my uniform that first night of class. To my relief, the students were most respectful, all addressing me as "Sir." They seemed engaged, and they did participate. I used the review of my syllabus to practice what we now call "TILT," transparency in learning and teaching, whereby I delineated not only all of the course requirements but also what I believed the students would need to do to meet expectations. I also reviewed the values, such as respect for all class members, that were to underlie our classroom conduct.

After 4 to 6 weeks of my Friday-night excursions, I found my anxiety gradually receding and ultimately disappearing altogether—and being replaced by a powerful sense of optimism in anticipation of the pleasure I was about to receive. It didn't take long for me to experience an epiphany that would change my life forever. It was dawning on me that I really loved the classroom experience, communication, give and take, affirmation, feedback, and the giving to students all I had of my concern, interest, encouragement, and joy in seeing their progress and discovery of new ways of thinking. And this realization came upon me: College teaching was giving me the opportunity to do the four things I loved the most to do: (a) talk; (b) read; (c) write; and (d) help people. This was so much fun it was even better than sex, and it definitely lasted much longer! And all my activities were integrated and dependent on each other. In order to "talk" (lecture) in class, I had to have read something. I loved to read, but it had never occurred to me that there was an occupation that would pay me to read! To be able to lecture, I had to take what I had read and reduce it to writing for my classroom lecture notes on proverbial yellow legal pad paper. Thus, this was my first monetary compensation for writing or speaking. The combination of reading, writing, and speaking was enabling me to do what I did in the psychiatric clinic only in a different delivery mode: help people. And so here I was, earning a legal living by doing the four things I knew I loved most to do.

My students were, frankly, astonishing. Admittedly, they were woefully underprepared for college, not because of any "fault" of their own, but rather the fault of the secondary school system of which they were products. Yes, some of them were males like me who were in college to receive a draft deferment—a perfectly legitimate motivation that I fully understood. But the majority were there on what they hoped would be a journey for upward social mobility to a life beyond working in the mills in their own community. While undereducated, they were intellectually curious and open to new ways of looking at things—not all of them, but many. And they were definitely intelligent. Most importantly, they were courageous risk takers, undertaking something most all of their parents had never done. They knew there was a real risk of failure, but they were there anyway. And most importantly, they inspired *my* mission to be a lifetime college educator in service to those less fortunate than me. I knew I had finally discovered my purpose. Everything I had experienced in life, especially my own initially miserable college experience, coupled with my transformative learning in the Air Force, had prepared me for this life-changing insight and resolution.

During that first term of teaching, I discovered a practice that had brought students and professors together for bonding in out-of-class settings for hundreds of years, namely, "drinking" after class. I use that word guardedly as my drinking was quite constrained. For one thing I had a 65-mile drive back late at night from Lancaster to Shaw AFB, and the Air Force did not tolerate its personnel like me violating civilian norms. But I confess, I regularly met after class with both male and female students (in groups, never alone) who wanted to socialize while talking further about what we had been discussing in class. Largely gone are those days, of course. At that time, the legal drinking age was 18, which legalized and normalized our behavior. This would come to an end 18 years later in 1985. But it did enable me to get to know my students much better and to learn more about their real lives in this archetypal mill town.

USC's College of General Studies, which administered the extension campuses, all eight of them, had other plans for me. Starting that summer after my first term of teaching at Lancaster, I was appointed as an adjunct instructor for the campus's on-base program at my very own Shaw AFB. Those courses were only 8 weeks long, 2 hours a night, 2 nights a week. And for the rest of my tour, I was teaching two courses every 8 weeks, occupying my Monday through Thursday evenings. Friday nights still belonged to the Lancaster campus. Starting that next fall term, the university dispatched me south, this time about 45 miles below the base to another county seat and its regional hospital in Orangeburg. There the university was sponsoring a nursing program, and I was needed to teach the Introduction to Sociology course and did so on Saturday mornings. In this era, USC was on a mission, specifically to "extend" higher education to South Carolina's smallest, rural communities. This also was something exciting to be part of.

All my adjunct settings were different, of course. My students on the base were mostly males. They were all on active military duty with the exception of a few female military dependents. The career NCOs, who were considerably older than me, were much more traveled than I, having served all over the world. I found my military students to be the most tolerant of my career when it came to matters of race, ethnicity, and political points of view; the mill culture of my students in Lancaster yielding the most conservative of my students. The military students as a cohort truly defied all my stereotypical biases learned in the higher education setting about how conservative "military minds" were. And unlike some of my civilian students, the military students were always prepared for class, being much more respectful of what authority figures ordered them to do. And, of course, my nursing students were highly goal oriented.

Teaching in the Terrible Year of 1968

My teaching experiences were to be even more momentous for me in the spring term of 1968 as the country was being torn apart by the war in Vietnam, the civil rights movement, and the tumultuous 1968 election. For me, the term began with the largest class of my teaching experience at Lancaster, about 80 students, still on a Friday night. I had to be scheduled in a large auditorium. In my first class I was to face one of the greatest challenges of my classroom teaching career. This was a historic year for the campus. It was being racially integrated by one male Black student, and I had the privilege of having that student in my very own classroom. I was here taking part in a moment of history. The campus, the community, and its people would never be the same now that this door had been finally opened. I was so excited to have him in my class. But he sat in the very back row, head down, baseball cap pulled down over his eyes, making it impossible for me to have eye contact with him.

During the first class, after reviewing the syllabus, which had included my usual exhortation that we all respect our fellow students, I asked the students if any of them had any questions. A large, White, male, sitting in the front row, put up his hand and inquired, "Yes, sir, I want to know what *you* think of us having to have n_____ in our class?" Realizing that I had just been pitched what was the greatest challenge of my very short teaching career, I knew this was the whole ball game for me with this class. I could be about to lose the whole thing. So, I thought I would try to finesse the guy. I replied to him, as I walked over to stand in front of him, looking down and frowning: "I don't believe I quite heard you. Would you care to repeat your question?" I was hoping against hope he would "get it" that I was really signaling disapproval of what he had asked. It didn't work. He then replied, "Yes, sir, I want to know what *you* think of us having to have n_____ in our class?" My response: "I heard you this time, and I need to tell you that your question has just violated a basic norm of this class that we will respect the dignity and worth of all our fellow students. I hope I am making clear that what you just said violated that norm. Now do you have any other questions?" And to my horror, he repeated his original question.

This time my response was, addressing him by name as respectfully as I could, "Look you need to understand I am an Air Force-trained killer, and I am ordering you to stand up and get out of this classroom right now, and if you don't, I will forcefully remove you!" Of course, this was all bluff and bravado on my part. I had no idea or plan for what I would do if he didn't do as I requested. But . . . he did. Whew. Somehow, I had survived that challenge and muddled through. I guess a light had come on and reminded me of a mantra among my fellow officer training candidates of 18 months previously, which was "fake it and make it!" I had faked it and made it. I have thought in retrospect of what my fallback position would have been had that kid just sat there. Would I have asked the other students to help me remove him? Who knows? Thankfully it never came to that. And he never returned to the course. The class was mine, all mine, from that moment on, except for one student about a month later, a female, who, after I had returned all the essay exams to the class, walked up in front of the class, threw her "bluebook" exam paper in my face, screamed at me that she had deserved an A, and stormed out of the room to the astonishment of all, especially me. Yes, she needed an anger management course, but I wasn't going to teach it.

For all of us in the military, that February was a shock. It was the month of the infamous Tet Offensive in South Vietnam. We had been hearing from our commanders for several years that we were "winning," the increasing draft and troop levels notwithstanding. But within the military we knew it was bad and that our valiant troops were not "winning" at all. My male students were no dummies. They could feel the heat of the draft on their necks increasing. In fact, the local draft board had increased its quotas and was enforcing a criterion for granting continuing deferments, that of a B average for the eligible students enrolled at our campus. So, for the first and only time in my life I was begged for higher grades to keep some of these young men out of the war. And I knew this was indeed within my ability to influence. This was a huge moral conundrum for me. My decision: I refused to honor such requests and rationalized that my students were responsible for their grades, not me, as I, too, had lost my graduate student deferment back in 1966. I had true empathy for their circumstance. I did talk to them about their alternatives, such as not waiting for the draft to get them and put them in the infantry, but volunteering and enlisting in a branch where the odds of survival were greater, just as I did. I never knew how many chose my route.

Witnessing History: The Orangeburg Massacre

February was also the month where I was a witness to one of the greatest tragedies of racial injustice in U.S. history, now known infamously as the Orangeburg Massacre thanks to a book of that title coauthored by one of my former colleagues, journalist Jack Bass. This occurred on February 8, 1968, in the small, rural South Carolina, county seat of Orangeburg, which is home to two of South Carolina's historically Black colleges and universities: South Carolina State College (now university—the public Black land-grant university) and Claflin College (now University), a private, Methodist-affiliated institution. This was 4 years after the Civil Rights Act, banning racial discrimination in public settings, had been enacted. On this particular evening a crowd of approximately 200 students from these two institutions gathered outside of a bowling alley in Orangeburg that was denying them entrance to exercise their legal right to bowl. The local police concluded they could not handle a crowd of this size, and so they called for reinforcements from the South Carolina Highway Patrol that arrived in force. In short order the Highway Patrol opened fire on the students, and 33 of them were shot, all in the back, killing three. The dead and the wounded were brought to the Orangeburg Regional Hospital, where I happened to be teaching my Introduction to Sociology course that very night.

This evening became my introduction to violent racial injustice. In the aftermath, any naïveté I had about the use of police power in the South against minorities was forever destroyed. These law enforcement officers were acquitted by an all-White state jury, and then indicted, but not con-victed again, by a federal jury in South Carolina. The officers were charged, not with murder this time, but with violation of civil rights under the 14th Amendment of 1868. But this was an impetus for Congress to act, and it adopted the Omnibus Crime Control Act of 1968 to provide law enforcement and National Guard training in crowd control. This would help prevent college students from being shot at the next student riot in South Carolina that happened on May 11, 1970, but would not prevent the killings that same month of two students at Jackson State University (Mississippi) and four students at Kent State University in Ohio.

A Principled Resignation

At the national level, things deteriorated further when on April 4, 1968, in Memphis, Tennessee, Martin Luther King Jr. was murdered. This was on a Thursday, and I was to teach at the Lancaster campus the next night. I decided I could not just proceed with my original lesson plans for that evening. I went to the Shaw AFB library and found several of King's books, including his most recent: *Where Do We Go From Here?* (which was also my question). In class that night I had the students join me in reading a number of passages aloud to be followed by reflection and discussion and also to be followed by complaints about me, as I would soon learn.

The following week when I arrived on campus for my next class, there was a note in my box to see the campus dean (CEO). I did so and was given one of the most astonishing and life-changing homilies of my life. He explained to me that after my class the preceding Friday when we honored King, that he, the dean, had been visited by a "delegation" of very unhappy students telling him I was a "n____ lover" who should not be tolerated. He criticized me for straying from the academic subject matter at hand, an argument I did not accept given the discipline of sociology's relationship to race relations. But beyond this he used this occasion to order me to tone down my anti–Vietnam War "rhetoric" in class, which had also come to his notice. The dean was a PhD U.S. Civil War historian himself and a World War II Army colonel. Of course, I reminded him that I was currently on active duty and that I had volunteered for military service just as he had. I also explained that many of the male students were very concerned about the threat to them of being drafted and being sent to Vietnam. That was the trigger for the most memorable part of this object lesson from my superior.

The dean explained to me what I already knew, of course, that draft quotas were rising rapidly, and that more and more local "boys" were being summoned for mandatory testing on the AFQT and physical examinations. Because of the history of educational and health-care discrimination against Black citizens, proportionately more of them than local White men were failing to meet the induction criteria. Hence, he explained to me, the level of anxiety for my White males was very high, and it was inevitable that many of them were going to be drafted, put in the infantry, sent to Vietnam, where some of them were going to be killed. So, now came the punch line: I was *not* to speak to my students about the realities of what was going on in our conduct of the war because many of them were going to be killed. We needed to persuade them this was a just cause and that lives were not being lost in vain. Bottomline: John, do *not* be factual with what you report to your students. I left this conversation saying only that I "understood" his request but not that I would honor it. He noted that. What was I to do?

This was not just a matter of how I was going to get through the last few weeks of the term having been now given a direct order from my supervisor to lie to my students. This development now posed a major dilemma for my future after my military service, which was scheduled to end in October. Because I had loved my teaching at USC Lancaster, I had been made an offer, by this same man who was now violating my academic freedom, and I had accepted a full-time teaching position effective in about 4 months. How in good conscience could I continue to teach in this unacceptable academic environment? The lesson here for me was an important life and career one: What do you do when your moral values are incompatible with the person(s) who supervises you and/or the organization you work for?

My decision was to resign from the position I had accepted from USC Lancaster, which I did immediately. Here I was, about to get out of the military with no job, but thankfully no debt, some money saved, and no dependents. I was grateful for all that I had learned from my teaching experiences for the university's extension division in the College of General Studies.

For chapter discussion questions, click the link or scan the QR code to visit Appendix C of the Online Compendium.

https://styluspub.presswarehouse.com/uploads/5e35cd13add3605ede5537f a2a5159aac11d5b57.pdf

PART THREE

BECOMING WHO I AM AS AN INTERNATIONAL HIGHER EDUCATION LEADER

U p until this point in both my personal and professional chronology, I have been attempting to set stage for the main event. I have endeavored to illustrate how I, as a person born into privilege, went my own ways after that advantaged beginning to prepare myself for a career in pursuit of justice for all undergraduate students, but especially for those less fortunate than I had been. It is not easy for some people, including myself, to make a reasonably objective and factual assessment as to what constitutes the most consequential and productive period of a leader's professional life. But this section is definitely the heart of the matter: tracing how I lost my first higher education position due to my civil rights activities, and then moving on to learn from all my life lessons to have a 3-decades'-long career at one research university from which I managed to lead both a national and international crusade to improve the beginning higher education experience.

I also relate the cofounding with my new wife, Betsy Barefoot, of a second higher education organization to support fellow educators pursuing the goal of student success. The material in Part Three literally covers a 52-year span from 1970–2022, which also closely mirrors the history of the now 50-year evolution of the widely replicated USC initiative, University 101, which I led for 25 years.

I believe that many of the actions I took are replicable by others, hopefully, readers of this book and that further adaptations of my work are more needed than ever today to increase student success. Thus, in this section I am laying the groundwork for the long-term institutionalization of the innovations with which I have been associated.

7

MY FIRST FULL-TIME
TEACHING POSITION:
LEARNING FROM IT, LOSING
IT, AND MOVING ON

Winthrop College for "The Fairest Flowers in the Southland"

After taking the bold step of resigning a position without having a new one to replace it, I wrote probably 30 to 40 institutions seeking an appointment. And I received a nibble, ironically, from the one geographically nearest, about 25 miles away. This was Winthrop College in Rock Hill, South Carolina, the state's all-female, regional comprehensive public institution of about 4,000 women. Founded in 1895, Winthrop still termed its students, "the Fairest Flowers in the Southland!" I was interviewed for a 1-year temporary appointment as instructor of history.

It has often been observed that growth can and does come from failure and suffering sometimes. This will be illustrated by my first full-time college teaching experience and my simultaneous journey as a civil rights advocate who was fired because of such activities. It is certainly the case that I would not have had nearly the same impact on higher education had I not lost my first job, learned from it, and gone on to a meaningful career at a much different, thankfully, kind of institution.

A Good First Year of Full-Time College Professing

The most notable moment in the interview with the dean of the faculty was when he said to me (remember this was 1968) "Ah, Mr. Gardner, I note that

91

you are single . . . ah . . . ah, well, tell me, do you like girls?" As a 25-year-old, heterosexual bachelor, I assured him I did. And to demonstrate my commitment, I commented on the pulchritude of a student who happened to walk by in our presence. He went on to explain to me, "Every single, unmarried, male faculty member who has come here that I can recall has ended up marrying a student." As I was later to learn, the institution was highly tolerant of such relationships but not for departures from established political norms of the community. I was offered—and accepted—the position.

The first of my 2 years at Winthrop was a unique one in the institution's history and its last for single-gender status. The administration was lobbying the South Carolina General Assembly to move to coeducational status, which the Alumni Association was fighting with messages such as the bumper stickers that read "Winthrop: Co-Ed = Co-Bed!" As I eventually came to understand the dynamics, the objection was not really to admitting men in general. It was really about allowing *Black* men to have proximity to those fairest flowers in the southland. The measure was ultimately adopted, and so my first year there was my only opportunity to experience single-gender higher education.

Moving on a Wednesday from a base of 8,000 male troops to a college of 4,000 women on Thursday was quite a shock to my system. The very first week as a civilian again, while walking across campus, I saw my dean approaching me. Quite unconsciously, I shifted my briefcase from my right hand to my left and raised the now free right hand to extend a crisp salute to my dean. It all happened so fast that he didn't even notice. But I did. It sunk in that the Air Force had really done a number on me, mostly good, over just 2 short years. Another adjustment I had to make was simply what was I going to wear on any given day. At Winthrop, unlike Shaw AFB, there was no official "uniform of the day." My uniform gradually changed to 1968 garb of bell bottom trousers, stylish cowboy boots, and a wide belt with a peace symbol buckle. And I could let my hair grow and relatively soon had a fine pair of sideburns. The Air Force–issued eyeglasses became passé too. The students reacted favorably to my new appearance.

During this first year, I loved my teaching. Because there were no male students, the female students could reveal how smart they really were and were quite engaged intellectually. Also, in the absence of males, the women felt free to skip makeup and often came to 8 o'clock classes in trench coats covering nightwear, with heads wrapped to cover their hair curlers. All this changed in my second year when the college entered a period of what was officially deemed "trial coeducation" including a first class of only 150 first-year males. But that's all it took; 150 men joining 4,000 women caused the women to adopt their familiar roles as conventional southern females conforming to male expectations. It was a disappointing development.

My teaching schedule was 4 days, with no classes for me on Wednesday. With all this "free time," I approached the Rock Hill Mental Health Center to "volunteer" my services, and they accepted me to do intake interviews on Wednesdays—all based on my military experience (unthinkable today given that my graduate degree was not in social work or another related mental health field and instead in American studies). I enjoyed working with a 100% civilian population and a broader age-range distribution than I had seen in the Air Force. The biggest difference was that I was not treating anxious people both before going to and then coming back from Vietnam.

By the end of my first year, I had become very popular as a new, young faculty member, and my single marital status probably helped me in that regard. I also was well liked by my faculty colleagues, my department chair, and dean. I was noted as unusual because of my military experience in general and in particular my military occupational specialty. At that time, the college, even though it had 4,000 students did not have even one professional counselor for student mental health issues. In today's climate, that seems almost incomprehensible, but that was the reality. Consequently, a number of faculty who came to know me referred some of their students to me for unofficial counseling. I found all of my teaching and advising interactions with my students very fulfilling. My initial direction developed in the Air Force to pursue a career in college teaching was being strongly confirmed. Okay, first year, so far so good.

As the second term progressed, I was offered a special appointment for summer school duties, a rare opportunity for an untenured junior faculty member like me. This opportunity was to serve as an instructor and "director of counseling" in a federally funded TRIO program awarded to Winthrop, Upward Bound. This was to be one of my most formative experiences in helping me be an effective and empathetic equity champion for college students over the next 50 years.

What was and is Upward Bound? The grant funded the participation of approximately 100 local high school–age sophomores, juniors, and seniors for participation. They were a racially mixed, predominantly Black group, but all had in common their meeting federal poverty guidelines for family incomes. The goal of Upward Bound was to both motivate and prepare them to pursue higher education. They came to the college for three summers of a residential program of instruction, counseling, field trips, socializing, and health care such as dental services. My role included being an instructor, director of advising/counseling, and living on campus in a residence hall with these 50 highly energetic males. There was never an 8-week period in my life in which I was so sleep deprived. But I had a ball. I really got into it, including the student dances for which they taught me the moves. I was hip—at least as any White man could be! This was to be my first Upward Bound experience, which I ultimately was blessed to have for 4 more years at USC.

It was by living with these students that I came to learn so much more about what their experiences had been growing up poor in South Carolina and attending what for the Black kids were vastly inferior racially segregated schools. I learned the unique meaning of "community" for Black citizens for which I could find no exact counterpart in any White culture I had experienced. I also saw how students saw "the police" differently than I did and how they had been largely unchallenged by their secondary school teachers who had such low expectations of them. In this respect, it was about 30 years later when I met at a social function one of my former Upward Bound students who by then had become a family physician in Columbia, Dr. Gary Bell. He told me that when he was 16 in my Upward Bound class, I was the first teacher who had ever asked him to write anything! Of course, the unstated assumption prior to his class with me was both that he had nothing of value to say and write and that he would never need to use writing to earn his living.

During that summer of 1969, the outside world of social protest worked its way into the Upward Bound student community. A young Black activist, "Redfearn Deuce," came to Rock Hill from Columbia to spend time (without an invitation) with these Upward Bound students. His presence was viewed by the college administration as an attempt to "radicalize" the students, and they were correct in that interpretation. Redfearn would argue that he was only trying to educate the students to the reality of being poor and Black in South Carolina. I attended most all of his sessions and heard things said about White people that I had never heard spoken in my presence before. In reality, I realize now he was teaching the students critical race theory. I needed to hear these things to better understand the appropriate anger and resentment I saw being directed to me based on the color of my skin. The college finally banned this "outsider" from the campus and took out a warrant against him for trespassing. I was called as a witness for the college in a magistrate's hearing, not one of my finer hours. I will never forget a forum the college president held with the students. In this setting he announced that they were henceforth not to be allowed to wear dashikis, which he described as "costumes." To this the students retorted that White men like him also wore "costumes," which consisted of white shirts and neckties! The president wasn't buying it. The end result of all this civil rights activism turmoil in the Upward Bound program was that the federal government sent a site inspector down who issued a finding that the college was definitely not acting toward the students in the spirit the funder had intended. The program grant was defunded and terminated.

Overall, my first year at Winthrop was a success. And it was definitely a learning experience about the culture of the professoriate. Rank, status, and seniority were very important. Seniority mattered just as it had in the union shop where I had worked as a steelworker in the can company. Rank mattered, just as it had in the Air Force I had just left. Although we didn't have symbols of rank attached to our clothing, we were still all very rank conscious. For example, in composing an internal campus-directed memo, all faculty were to be listed in order of their faculty rank: the full professors, then the associates, and so forth. And within each rank, people were listed in order of length of service at that rank. This went so far as determining the processional ranks for convocations and commencement where each of us was assigned a number, which was the ultimate marker for status. Given my status, I came at the end of the processional. Also, as an untenured, nontenure-track eligible "instructor," I received the least desirable of everything that could be doled out on a discretionary basis: office space (I had to "share" an office); hours of teaching—I had eight-o'clock classes 4 days a week; committee assignments—I was made committee secretary of every one I served on. Another determinant of one's status was which faculty parties you were invited—or not invited to.

The academic year, 1968–1969, was a tumultuous one in national and state politics. And as a single, debt-free, liberal, male with a prized honorable discharge from the Armed Forces, I was as free as I ever had been in my still young life. In practical terms this meant that I was very active politically and never met a cause I didn't want to be connected to. In particular, there were two: I sought training as a conscientious objector counselor from the American Friends Service draft counseling program and actually served in such capacity across the state border in Charlotte, North Carolina; and I worked with another liberal professor to establish just what we thought a small southern town like Rock Hill needed: a local chapter of the American Civil Liberties Union. This was to be my ultimate downfall at staid Winthrop College.

Getting Fired for My Civil Rights Activism and Big Mouth

The fall term of 1969 began, and I was assigned to teach a large lecture session of some 350 students in world civilization history. I taught in Tillman Auditorium in the Tillman Administration building, named for a man who was surely the most racist governor in the history of South Carolina, Benjamin Tillman, the legislative founder of both Winthrop and Clemson University. I learned two lessons in that large lecture class.

The first was never teach a class after you have attended a faculty group luncheon at which a textbook salesman provided us with free pitchers of beer. I didn't think I had consumed excessively, but when I went to my large lecture class after lunch, I could definitely hear from the perfect amplification of my very sensitive microphone, that my voice didn't sound like a sober individual. And some of my students let me know they were amused. I was not in the least bit amused; to the contrary, I was profoundly embarrassed. Never again would I consume any alcohol prior to any public speaking event, and I haven't to this day.

Of far more consequence was something I did quite innocently—or so I thought. The college distributed an internal news bulletin each week called *The Green Sheet*. It contained announcements that we were encouraged to read aloud to our students. One such announcement was from the campus Presbyterian Student Center, hardly a leftist organization. The announcement that I read to the class was about a "free" film made by the American Civil Liberties Union about the Chicago Police Riot that had taken place the year before (August of 1968) at the Chicago National Democratic Convention. Unbeknownst to me, one of my 350 students in that lecture hall was the daughter of the chair of the college's board of trustees, who had some personal objections to the actions of the local ACLU chapter—the one I cofounded. A week or so later I was called in to see my department chair and issued a letter of nonrenewal of my second temporary appointment as instructor of history for the coming academic year. Gotta love this euphemism: "nonrenewed," an academic's way of saying "fired!" My chair explained exactly how this had been decided: The student in my class had gone home and reported to her daddy, the board chair, that the ACLU had been mentioned positively by one of her professors; the board chair then called the president and secured my termination. The president passed the message to the dean of the faculty, who then passed the decision on to my dean, my chair, and ultimately to me.

Of course, I was stunned, and angered. I really didn't understand how this could have happened to me. Naïvely, I thought I was playing by the rules my organization-man father had taught me were keys to success in organizational life. I had shown up on time for my classes. The students praised me. I got along well with my colleagues. I kept my boss informed, volunteered for extra assignments, and conscientiously pursued all that was requested of me. I was honest, law abiding, the works. But there had been a big missing gap in my father's tutelage: politics. And politics had prevailed. Dad never told me not to establish a local chapter of the ACLU that might take actions to offend prominent local citizens.

I debated whether to file some kind of legal action to claim violation of my academic freedom. But I had to accept that as untenured faculty member I really didn't have the requisite grounds, and that further, if I protested, the college would see that I was "blacklisted" for future employment. I finally rationalized that this college just wasn't good enough for me if it was to treat me in this manner. And I started looking for another job.

One of my mature evening students who had come to like and respect me had introduced me to her husband, who was a public school superintendent in a contiguous county. He actually offered me a job as an assistant superintendent even though I had no K–12 certification. The salary was to have been quite decent, $10,000 a year (compared to my salary then of $8,000). But realizing what I was coming to know about myself and how I didn't really fit with the views of the local political power structure, I concluded that taking such a job in a very rural county would just be asking for trouble. Simultaneously, I was offered an appointment as an instructor in USC's College of General Studies, starting the next fall for $8,500 for 9 months. My conclusion was that I would have a higher probability of retaining that position than the one as a rural public-school administrator at the height of the civil rights protest era.

This was a hugely important decision as it brought me back to USC, where I was finally able to fulfill my professional destiny. I had dodged another bullet as a Connecticut Yankee in the land of South Carolina. Just like my former Air Force supervisor, Dr. Reardon, had taught me, I was going to show that I could learn from experience and this time keep a job, even though I could be a tempting target in the state. But keep a job I did. As I look back at my 2 years at Winthrop, the most important insights I learned that helped me become a better college teacher and leader, especially as a champion for less advantaged students, were those I gained from my work in the Upward Bound TRIO program. That was an experience most White men like me would never have had, and I have been different and positively affected ever since. Thank you, Winthrop College, even though you fired me!

For chapter discussion questions, click the link or scan the QR code to visit Appendix C of the Online Compendium.

https://styluspub.presswarehouse.com/uploads/5e35cd13add3605ede5537f a2a5159aac11d5b57.pdf

8

ON REINVENTING
THE BEGINNING
YEAR OF COLLEGE

My Real Life's Work in The First-Year Experience

T here is no question that my reputation, credibility, expertise, and most important legacies, including inspiration for others who wish to become successful student success leaders, were all the outcome of 29 years of full-time service to the University (and the people) of South Carolina. In this chapter I will begin tracing the evolution of events leading from a student riot in 1970 to an international movement to transform the first year of higher education. This will be illustrated by tracing the development of the "first-year experience" movement and its archetypal example of a "first-year experience"–type program, University 101, and an associated international conference series and set of publishing activities to broaden that impact. This is also a case study of innovation at both the individual and institutional level and offers many illustrations for replication. The timing of my writing about this is *not* coincidental with the fact that the 2022–2023 academic year is the 50th anniversary of the now fabled University 101 program.

I am going to assume that most people who are aware of the full scope of my career would likely conclude that my most important work was done at USC during the period 1974–1999 when I was the founding executive director of the University 101 programs and the National Resource Center for The First-Year Experience and Students in Transition. It is this work that my entire life and work up to this point had prepared me to do, and it is this work that is my enduring legacy to higher education. Much of what I did was made possible by others and is being carried on by others. I hope my story shows that you, too, can work with others to do important work in our field.

It All Began With a Riot

After being fired from Winthrop College in the fall of 1969 and finishing out the balance of that academic year, I started my new position at USC in Columbia in September of 1970. Unbeknownst to me, the precipitating event for the foundational experience of what became my life's work, the redesign of the beginning college experience, had occurred 4 months before in May of 1970 in the form of a tumultuous student protest on the campus.

The immediate catalyst for this was the U.S. so-called "incursion" into Cambodia in early May 1970, leading to campus protests around the country, including those at Jackson State University in Mississippi and Kent State University in Ohio, where collectively six students died. In South Carolina the governor, when faced with a similar protest, dispatched the National Guard, but unlike 27 months previously in Orangeburg, it was not the practice to shoot White college students. Instead, they were tear gassed. They dispersed and moved on to another location, to the university's administration building, where the board of trustees was meeting and where they eventually barricaded the president, Thomas F. Jones, in his office. The next day he held a press briefing and told the press, "The students have given me an extended opportunity to observe and reflect upon the meaning of student behavior!" The conclusions of his reflective process would become very clear to me 2 years later.

Formative USC Influences Before the Creation of University 101 in 1972

There were many very specific positive influences at USC on my preparation for what became my life's work. One early experience was teaching in a model TRIO Upward Bound program (unlike the one I taught in at Winthrop College, which was defunded by the federal government). At that time, TRIO was a set of three individual program initiatives, Upward Bound, Talent Search, and Student Support Services, that were overseen by the U.S. Department of Education and created as part of the Higher Education Act of 1965. These programs provide for low-income students a 3-year educational preparation and motivational process for going on to college (Upward Bound); assistance for high school students and their families in navigating the college choice process, especially for securing financial aid (Talent Search); and a highly structured first year of college framework for selected courses, advising, career planning, and providing of peer leaders (Student Support Service). I learned that the USC program had been the first TRIO grant awarded to a southeastern predominantly White institution because the university was willing to accept the federal requirements that all program activities be racially integrated. USC had been successful in securing grants to be funded for all three component programs that made up the larger TRIO umbrella. That alone made me proud. And to its credit the university put forward some of its best teaching faculty to be involved in the program. I was honored to be included.

Compared to most of my faculty colleagues, I was very junior and untenured. Most of my peers were distinguished colleagues at the full-professor rank. My work in the TRIO program at USC, and in particular Upward Bound, beginning in 1971, gave me a wonderful opportunity to teach with and learn from stellar senior faculty colleagues and also from local high school instructors, with whom I would normally never have interacted. The program was very interconnected to local community groups, which again, because of racial segregation I would not normally have interacted with.

The students were a joy to teach. I think what was most important for me as a young, developing faculty member was the fact that we had to teach and motivate our students without the proverbial carrot and stick: grades and academic credit. Rather, this was all about sparking genuine enthusiasm and skill development. We interacted with the students in and out of class, over meals, at their social activities, and on field trips. We met their families, and we learned their stories. We also learned about their community lives and their school experiences, which until the year before, 1970, had been racially segregated. Yes, the South Carolina courts and school systems had successfully delayed and avoided integration from the 1954 Supreme Court mandate of *Brown v. Board of Education* until the denial of the last appeal in 1970. Thus, early in my career I was able to observe firsthand the most severe consequences of separate and unequal public education for our children. These were children who had spent their entire precollege years in racially segregated schools and would potentially become my future college students.

Another important learning experience for me would fall under the heading of "learning how to get things done through academic committees." In 1971, I managed to get myself appointed to membership on the university's counseling services committee, and I was made committee chair even though I was still an untenured instructor. We were facing a key challenge: how to get students to seek assistance from helping services.

What we did was to launch a whole-new approach to marketing the availability of free counseling services. One of the ways we did this was by the development of a truly colorful, psychedelic-looking poster, ideally suited for display in residence hall rooms. To create this, we did an original design using university graphic artist work. Thankfully, we ran this mock-up prototype by a focus group of students who trashed it. So, we turned over the task of a new design to a student group, and the resulting poster became a huge hit on campus. We saw it all over campus, generally displayed voluntarily by students. Utilization of counseling services increased. Here was an important lesson: Get student input from the outset!

In 1971–1972 I had my very first career opportunity to bring a modicum of justice for the neglected student population of transfer students. Specifically, I was given a slot on a university task force (entitled Strategies for Change and Knowledge Utilization) to design a new bachelor's degree to solve a problem. That problem was the gross discrimination against students graduating from the state's two-year technical college associate-degree programs by not permitting them to transfer credits to the university's bachelor's degrees. Who were these students? They were students who did not have the money necessary to begin their college education at the university—students of color and first-generation students, disproportionately. This population also included military students and veterans who had served and lived in multiple locations but never long enough to accumulate enough college credits to earn a BA or BS, spouses of persons who had experienced frequent job relocations and who had likewise not been able to stay long enough anywhere to finish a degree, and finally students who had frequently changed their major and had curricular and life objectives that were just not fitting into traditional degree requirements. This was all about a curricular design that would generously accommodate transfers from lower-status two-year, nonresidential institutions and who were less advantaged than our four-year residential students.

To address this situation, we created a new degree, the Bachelor of Arts in Interdisciplinary Studies (BAIS), approved by the USC Faculty Senate in 1972. This was revolutionary, almost heretical. Now it was possible for a student to complete a bachelor's degree with a minimum of just 30 hours in residence at the upper division (junior and senior level). The students were required to spend the last year only in residence and maintain a minimum 2.0 average. There were no fixed required courses as long as the student's program of study was approved by a team of two academic advisors (who were faculty). This was a true democratization of the curriculum and provided greater access to university four-year degree education. Although the impetus for the creation of this degree was to serve transfer students, the degree was also open to nontransfer students, those who had originally matriculated at USC but had not been able to meet their objectives in an existing discipline-focused degree major.

I was so proud to be part of this creative force. This was also my first introduction to the two types of students in U.S. higher education, the transfer student and the nontransfer student, and I recognized how grossly unequal these two types of student experiences were. Now, 50 years later, a major focus of my work and writing is about improving the nation's attention to transfer students. For the entirety of my remaining time at USC, from 1972 to 1999, I served as a faculty advisor in the BAIS degree program. This gave me some of the most creative academic advising opportunities of my career. And to bring this home to my family, one of my two sons, who was not a transfer student, chose and successfully completed the BAIS as his preferred route to a bachelor's degree—a route that combined for him the disciplines of business and philosophy.

During the 1971–1972 year I became an innovator for that time in using technology to provide alternative opportunities to teach students. No one who knows me now would ever believe I was or could ever be a technology innovator, but I was in this period. Very simply, what I did was to put two of my real-time courses on prerecorded video-cassette tapes to make the content accessible for students at flexible times of their choosing. Yes, in 1971–1972 this was real rocket science. And I also made the same two courses available through what we then termed "correspondence studies," whereby students submitted and received all their assignments returned by me via the U.S. mail. While this was a well-established U.S. higher education practice at that time, it was not an option I had ever experienced in undergraduate or graduate school.

What I didn't know then, but I do know now, is that in every organization there is usually a small community of innovators who attract and learn from each other. Without realizing it, by the end of my first 2 years at USC, I was beginning to develop a reputation as a young faculty innovator, a concept that some cynics believed to be an oxymoron. In my regular teaching I was also able to innovate, such as in use of experiential learning principally through field trips. And I discovered one type of nontraditional student I certainly never had encountered in my own undergraduate school: an incarcerated student, released on his own recognizance, to take courses on the USC campus even though almost a decade before he had killed his spouse. He ended up meeting a student in one of my courses and they eventually married, a ceremony I attended. Some years later, he named me the executor of his will. He is alive as I write and still in touch with me after his law-abiding life. Oh, how we get engaged in the lives of our students.

At the end of the 1971–1972 academic year, I was promoted from instructor to assistant professor and taught for a second summer in Upward Bound. By then I was ready for the phone call that was going to change my life.

All It Took Was One Phone Call

On a typical hot South Carolina summer day in July 1972, 1 month after the Watergate burglary, I went to a local restaurant, ironically named "The Winners' Circle," for lunch. I had left word in my office where I could be reached, and while there I was interrupted with a call. A woman's voice came on the line introducing herself as the university president's executive assistant. I even remember her name to this day, Elaine Graff. She instructed me, "Hold for President Jones." My heart sunk. I asked myself, based on my prior record of being fired from another college as the result of a president's decision, "Is this how they nonrenew people here at USC with a presidential touch?"

This deep, booming, but recognizable voice came on the line—my university president, whom I had heard speak a number of times but who had never spoken to me or met me. His opening line was "John, this is Tom J, and I'm calling to ask you to do me a favor!"

Because this was a month after Watergate, everyone was thinking of the uses of presidential power. I quipped back to him, "Yessir, as long as it is not illegal or unethical!"

The president laughed and I felt slightly relieved. "John, I'd like you to attend a workshop."

"Yes, of course, Mr. President. What kind of workshop?"

"John, you don't need to know that right now; you will learn all about the workshop when you attend."

"Yes sir, I am a veteran of the Air Force, and I understand a command performance when I hear one!"

The president laughed.

"And John, if you like the workshop, I'd like you to teach a course for me!"

"Yessir, but what kind of a course?"

"John, you don't need to know that now. You will learn that in the workshop!"

"Yessir. I understand."

"And, John, I will be there with you for the workshop! You'll be getting more information. Thank you very much. See you there."

Even though I enjoyed an ever-increasing close relationship with President Jones until his death 9 years later in 1981, I never asked him or heard how he had learned of me and my work in the first place. I had never met him personally nor had any communication with him about anything. But, like all good leaders he had his own sources of information. I knew he had some kind of brain trust around this initiative, and I suspected that some of its members had heard something about my work. I had only been on the campus 2 years; I was very young (28) and very junior but already known as an innovator. However, I don't really know exactly what brought me to Jones's attention, and I never will.

This is also an example of a mantra I preach constantly to my staff (see Appendix D in the online compendium accompanying this book): "Everything is connected to everything else and everyone is connected to everyone else." I have learned and relearned many times how good works for others can come back in countless ways that you may not initially have anticipated.

First Steps in Designing University 101: A Story of Presidential Leadership

The information about the workshop soon arrived, and it was to be held in the president's lounge in the Williams-Brice Football Stadium. The workshop was scheduled to run for 3 weeks, five afternoons a week, 3 hours an afternoon. The purpose of the workshop was to design a three–credit hour course, University 101, "The Student in the University." We were to learn later that the total number of hours to be invested in the workshop was exactly the same number students would ordinarily spend in a three–credit hour course; hence we would both participate in and observe the kind of group process that could actually occur in this new course. President Jones did attend, and oh did he participate. He was there with us every day, 5 days a week, 3 hours an afternoon for 3 weeks.

I came to learn that this workshop was an outgrowth of the work of a study committee that had been convened by President Jones after the student riot of May 1970. The committee had worked for 2 years to determine the cause(s) of the riot and to make recommendations to prevent such from reoccurring. There were 25 participants in the workshop; seven or eight were members of the Division of Student Affairs, and the rest of us were faculty. The faculty ranged from very junior, nontenured faculty like me to some real heavy hitters.

Apparently, the committee was unable to come up with a substantive vision for doing what Jones wanted to do: Transform the university culture to make it more, in the language of the 21st century, "student centered." Jones then, his patience exhausted, took matters into his own hands, a risky thing for a university president to do, and offered a proposal for faculty governance consideration to create this new course. As he later explained it to me, the riot had led him to think that these very traditional, God-fearing, respectful, polite, largely Baptist students had not come to the university angry. But something had happened to make them angry. We had obviously done something to them! This actually was a very novel way of thinking because it held the university responsible for a student outcome, namely anger toward the university. Jones further believed that attitudes were taught and learned and that theoretically you can teach human beings to think anything, do anything. So, in the parlance of the early 1970s, why not teach them to love the university instead of hating it? How then could you teach new students to love the university upon entry? That became the charge to this new University 101 course. After Jones delivered his proposal to the Faculty Senate for this new course in July of 1972, the senate gave a 1-year approval. The next question then became *who* should teach the students to love the university?

Jones firmly believed that it was the role of the faculty to teach students. But he realized that faculty by both inclination and training were subject-matter experts and had never had any instruction on pedagogy, particularly some kinds of teaching that might lead students to love the institution. So, he came upon this radical idea that we could design a required special faculty development experience that would be linked to the course—and that was the faculty development workshop that he invited me to attend.

Jones was drawing on an already well-established curricular genre in the U.S. undergraduate curriculum, a course type dating to 1882 (note that's 1882, not 1982), generically known as a "first-year seminar." The ultimate arbiter for legitimacy in U.S. higher education, Harvard University, had offered such a course since 1959. Some 18 years later I and my USC colleague, Betsy Barefoot, had the privilege of interviewing the founder of Harvard's seminar, distinguished professor of sociology and higher education, David Riesman, the author of one of those two books I was required to read as punishment in my first year of college.

But what was unique about this USC first-year seminar was that it represented both a public and a hidden agenda. The public agenda was that it was a course for students in which they would be taught how to function in a university environment, learn all about the purposes of that environment for their own self-improvement, have a positive beginning experience, come to love the university, and not riot in the future. Note that there was no public discussion or rationale put forward that this course was to be about "retaining" students" (that was only to be discovered in 1975, 3 years later, when research found that participation in University 101 correlated positively with a higher retention rate of University 101 participants than nonparticipants). The hidden agenda, however (that is, hidden by the president) was that there were really to be two courses: one for students and one for faculty. And the one for faculty was to be this mandatory, faculty development experience prior to their first teaching of University 101. A tradition was to be established that no one would ever teach this course without having gone through this preparation experience, a tradition honored to this very day now 50 years later.

Jones's vision was that to humanize the university environment for students, faculty had to be given formal pedagogical instruction in humanistic teaching strategies. And his thinking was if faculty "got" this treatment and it really "took," even if they taught University 101 only once, the impact of the more generic faculty development process would affect how they interacted with their students in other disciplinary and interactional settings. Thus, as time went by, more and more faculty would receive this humanistic development experience. This would change the culture of the university, making it more humane and student centered. Since that first workshop in 1972, we have continued to bring new educators into the University 101 pipeline, with significant effect on the university culture, particularly with respect to the priority of providing students an excellent, humane, supportive "first-year experience." And the original practice of requiring the University 101 training as a prerequisite for teaching the course has been maintained, without exception, for the past 50 years.

Another part of Jones's vision was that the faculty couldn't do this all by themselves and that they would benefit from relationships with a relatively new professional subset, members of the embryonic "student affairs" profession. That is why student affairs professionals were in that very first training workshop. Ultimately, I was to learn that their presence had been sealed in a deal between the president and his vice president for student affairs, Charles "Chuck" Witten, the first educator to be so titled in the history of the university. The deal went like this: In exchange for contributing 16 professional student affairs staff members as University 101 instructors for 16 sections a year, the Division of Student Affairs would get one new staff slot from the president's budget. That slot went to hire a new full-time PhD-level counselor for the counseling center. And for my entire 25-year period as course director the occupant of that slot never chose to teach University 101. Sometimes in higher education we are afflicted by lack of big-picture thinking and/or gratitude. But that's an inconsequential, largely unknown fact in the history of this innovation. What really mattered was the course was launched.

What did we do in that original University 101 Faculty Development Training Workshop? In brief, we designed the goals, broad objectives, learning objectives, content, and pedagogy for a course that has been sustained for 50 years. We learned all kinds of information about group dynamics, the human potential movement and pedagogy, student development theory, holistic learning and development, experiential learning, the potential for faculty/student affairs partnerships, and all kinds of other things that I had never thought or heard of before. We used this 45-hour workshop model to simulate the phases of group development our actual classes could and would experience. And the 25 of us had formed new and some very significant professional and personal relationships. I had about 5 years' teaching experience by then but had never had any kind of professional faculty development support and training. My own teaching would never be the same again.

My First University 101 Class

Thanks to that one phone call the course was launched with 17 sections, and I was to teach one of them. It was the most memorable teaching experience of my young life. I had 20 students (we now cap enrollment at 19 to positively correlate with the *U.S. News and World Report* ranking criteria algorithm). With respect to those students, a USC colleague reached out to me several years ago and sent me a photocopy of the grade report I had submitted on those students to our registrar for that fall semester 1972 and asked me if I could recall any of the 20 students. I remembered three. One was the only Black student in the class. I remember the little town where she was from, just north of Savannah in very rural South Carolina. One day she told our class that there were more people living in her residence hall at USC than lived in her hometown! That really grabbed me and the whole class. What happened to her? She became a pediatrician.

The second student I remembered was a university policeman, whom I had met out at the Columbia airport, which had a lovely pond where I used to take my Chesapeake Bay retriever to swim and retrieve decoys. This officer, then an airport policeman on patrol, came to know me, and I eventually talked him into becoming a USC part-time student. He also eventually became a house sitter for me when I was a single parent and needed an adult in the house, armed and dangerous, guarding my teenage son from all the things he might have foolishly done while his father was away. This former student remained a close friend of mine and my family until his death in 2022. One year, when I chaired the entire university's annual in-house charitable foundation drive, I learned that his contribution was the largest of any individual USC faculty or staff member as a percent of his USC base salary!

The third student I remembered was Darla Moore, the only highly successful female business leader in the United States for whom a school of business accredited by the Association to Advance Collegiate Schools of Business (AACSB) is named in recognition of her extraordinary philanthropic support—her initial $25 million gift to the USC business school. While I can't take any credit for her post-USC success, I can claim that at least I wasn't a contributor to a bad experience that caused her to drop out of the university. The moral of the story is that we *never* know who is in our classes in terms of whom they are going to become.

As I taught this class once a week in a 3-hour time block, as soon as possible after class, I would write in a journal my reflections on what had transpired between the students and me and the impact of that particular class on my insights into college students and effective college teaching. I am just sick that somehow over my 32-plus years at USC I lost this journal. But that was long after I submitted it to President Jones at the end of the semester. I did so because he had reached out to each of the 17 University 101 instructors stipulating a report from each of us about the outcomes from our first teaching of University 101. I submitted to him a copy of my journal to constitute that report. He also had appointments made for each of us to come to his office and to personally receive from him a $500 stipend, covered by funds from a Ford Foundation Venture Fund grant that he had been awarded to support innovation at the university. I will always remember my conversation with him. He had actually read parts of my journal, quoted some passages, and asked me for further commentary. I just couldn't believe the most powerful leader on "planet USC" was showing this level of interest in *my* work. Of course, what I was discovering was the power of his mentoring. This was a gift I would resolve to pass on to others.

Being Adopted by a Presidential Mentor

Teaching University 101 for the first time was not going to be the end of the developmental opportunities this president would provide me. I didn't have to wait long. Even before the first semester was over, President Jones had "persuaded" the deans to allow him to test out another experiment.

It was an expansion of a theme that started with what he had seen in the university's TRIO program, especially the Upward Bound component of TRIO. That theme was what can happen when you take the most dedicated and talented university faculty and staff and put them in instructional and leadership roles with the most disadvantaged students for all kinds of developmental experiences.

Jones had come to believe that the university was a vehicle for working the kind of magic that he had seen in TRIO but that would not be dependent on federal funding and also could operate at far larger scale. It was his belief that ultimately *all* entering university students could benefit from such experiences. After seeing how this could be advanced through University 101, Jones wanted to see whether University 101 humanistic pedagogies could be applied to students above the first-year level. Even beyond that he wanted to see if we could introduce professional education majors to these pedagogies so that when they became certified teachers we could expand the influence of this experiment beyond the university itself. He recruited me to teach an experimental course, Education 399, for teacher education majors, about 20 of them in the spring of 1973. As I recall, we offered about five sections, and I taught one of them. We saw the same kinds of impacts on student motivation and behaviors that we had seen with first-year students in University 101. Jones followed very closely the progress of his latest experiment and conceived of still another one. Thus, before that spring term ended, he invited me to be part of still another cohort of faculty teaching another experimental course.

This next course was to be offered in fall 1973 and was, again, a bootlegged University 101 adaptation, this time not for education majors, but instead for students who were being readmitted to the university after having been academically suspended, put on academic probation, or in a voluntary stop-out period but now returning to the university. For this venture, Jones got the faculty chair of the Department of Religious Studies to offer this course as Religion 399. I taught this again, and the third time was the charm. I came to recognize that University 101 was an adaptable, replicable model that could be applied to other undergraduate students who had at least one thing in common: some kind of shared transition in a group process, led by a former survivor of that same transition. In my case what I had in common with these students was my own experience of having been placed on academic probation and then successfully getting off probation so that I could continue and earn my bachelor's degree. In all of these adaptations, we would support the students and help them better understand and function in an academic transition period whether they were beginning college, beginning a major, or beginning again after a voluntary or involuntary absence.

Another Visit to the President's Office as His Third Choice

Six months later, in June of 1974, I received another call summoning me to the president's office. I had no idea what this was going to be about. I was 2 years into my assistant professor tenure-track appointment and exactly 30 years old. And I was about to have another transformative conversation with my mentor, President Jones. Only this time it was going to be in person and not on a telephone. The conversation went like this: "John, I'm going to be honest with you. I've asked you here to offer you a job, for which you are *not* my first choice. In fact, you are my third choice. But unlike you, my first two choices were tenured full professors. Both of them turned me down. However, I believe you would be ideal for this—our first official faculty leader for University 101!"

I was, of course, floored by this. I had not known that there was a "search" for such a position. I came to learn there was no search at all. This was a university president trying to ensure the survival of one of his most important pet initiatives 2 weeks short of his leaving office. I had been aware that after 12 years of service the president had lost a vote of confidence of his board. He had made plans to graciously move on and had accepted a position as vice president for research at his alma mater, the Massachusetts Institute of Technology (MIT). In a conversation with him 7 years later, he confided, "John, your friends they come and they go. But your enemies just accumulate!"

He had paid the ultimate price for defending student "radicals" 4 years previously in the riot period, thus alienating a number of very conservative, powerful, local political leaders, especially the local prosecutor, who viewed him as not tough enough against "outside agitators." But his ultimate sin was supporting a gift of a federal grant from a South Carolina congressman, William Jennings Bryan Dorn, who was chair of the U.S. House of Representatives Veteran's Affairs Subcommittee. Dorn offered a pork bonanza to provide a 7-year grant to USC to provide start-up funding to create a new and second medical school for the state of South Carolina. The stipulation was that this was to be a new and second medical school over and above the state's one existing medical school in Charleston. This new medical school was to be in the capitol city, Columbia, and was to be built on the grounds of the Veteran's Administration Hospital. This started a furor in the legislature with representatives from the state's "lowcountry," the Charleston environs, who were bitterly opposed to this effort for fear that it would ultimately siphon money from the original medical school in Charleston.

Ultimately, Jones won the battle but lost the war. He persuaded his board to accept the federal gift, but he lost his job in the process. His original vision had been that a poor state like South Carolina needed a second medical school that would have a different mission—producing family doctors who would be willing to locate to the state's rural areas and thus serve its poorer citizens. This was very much in keeping with other initiatives taken by Jones, originally from Mississippi himself. He was acutely aware of poverty and all its associated downsides, including racism; poor health, health care and nutrition; and inadequate public education. It was the same vision that led him to persuade state and city leaders to racially integrate the university peacefully with no state or federal troops and marshals and to establish the first graduate library school in the state to improve public school libraries that he believed were foundational for raising K–12 outcomes. I mention this because it was ultimately that college that would invite me, in 1983, to transfer my tenure and full professorship and join its faculty, an invitation I accepted.

I am aware enough to know that, in effect, I won this position to lead University 101 because there had been no open search, no affirmative action. Both the individuals who had been offered the position prior to me were also male and White. If there had been an official search, open to many potential applicants, there is good chance I would not have been selected. Of course, I can never know. But I do know that I resolved to lead this program to serve *all* students. And ultimately, we found we were having the most positive impact on our Black and low-income students.

The Power of Lifetime Mentor/Mentee Relationships

I am often, inappropriately, given credit for the creation of USC's University 101 course. That is not correct. I helped launch the course, but our president was really the prime mover. And by then he had also become my mentor, a role he played with continuing influence until his death in June of 1981. While I was also doing things on my own to institutionalize this experiment at USC and to replicate it at hundreds of other institutions around the globe, he was continuing to influence me. Primarily, he did so by staying in touch: written correspondence, occasional phone calls from him to ask me to do something—usually to send information on University 101 to someone and some institution he wanted to inspire with our example. He never took his foot off this pedal until he developed a terminal illness, but even in that situation he had a profound influence on me.

In the spring of 1981, I learned that President Jones was in decline and that he was nearing the end of his life. In talking about this with my dean, Harry E. "Sid" Varney, another mentee of President Jones, we were trying to decide whether we should plan to attend his eventual funeral. Then it occurred to us: Why should we wait until he died? Why not go see him while he still lived? I reached out to Jones's administrative assistant to arrange a visit to his office at MIT. The assistant relayed one request to us from Jones, namely, to determine beforehand what he would need to do to transfer his personal library to USC's library holdings. I made that inquiry and obtained the information he needed to execute this gift. I only needed to obtain the answer to this one, very simple, question: How many volumes would be gifted? Sid Varney and I got up very early one morning in June of 1981, flew to Boston, and arrived to his office about 11:00 a.m. Our first order of business, at President Jones's direction, was to use a tape measure and record the length of all the book shelving in his two MIT offices. Sid and I did the measuring and called out the linear board feet to Jones, who duly noted our numbers and punched them into this huge calculator on his desk. Then he took the gross number and, being the engineer he was, divided that total number by something to yield a calculation of how many volumes he would be dedicating to the USC libraries. I seem to remember it was around 11,000 volumes. And then it hit me: What we had been doing was performing a farewell ritual in which we had just measured the dimensions of his intellectual coffin.

President Jones then motioned for me and Sid to sit down with him, very closely, and for each of us to give him one hand. He had another ritual in mind, and that very simply was to ask me to swear an oath with my dean as my witness, that I would *never* give up the mission he had launched to disseminate the University 101 vision for the humanistic redesign of the beginning college experience. I tearfully took the oath, which I have recalled a number of times in my future when powerful people had other plans for me. Two years later in 1983, the university president, James Holderman, wanted me to become the next vice chancellor for regional campuses and continuing education for USC. I agreed on the condition that I be allowed to retain my directorship of the University 101 program. President Holderman and Chancellor John J. Duffy agreed, and I was able to honor my commitment to former President Jones. Three more times in my 32 years at USC I was offered positions that most would have leapt at. I did not, and stayed focused instead on the opportunity and mission that Jones had made possible for me and to which I was committed.

The Groundbreaking First Formal Evaluation of University 101

I knew there were many skeptics who predicted the demise of President Jones's "pet" program, University 101, after he lost his appointment as president and a new president came on board. A related prediction was that

I had been a foolish risk-taker in taking on the leadership role of University 101, which surely would have a short-term lease on professional life. About 10 weeks after the new and interim president, William H. Patterson, had assumed the reins, he spoke to the September 1974 meeting of the USC Faculty Senate. I just happened to be a faculty senator and so was there in the audience to hear him announce that one of the major efforts of his administration would be to examine the innovations of his predecessor to determine whether they should be sustained. Exhibit A, he announced, was to be University 101. In retrospect, I found it noteworthy that he did *not* use the word "assess," but as I came to learn, that is exactly what he had in mind. There I was, 2.5 months into my new job as an untenured assistant professor, hearing the president telling a live audience as my witnesses that my program could be on the chopping block. That didn't happen, although I couldn't have known that at the time.

Now, I commend President Patterson for the fairness and thoroughness of the actions he took. The first thing he did was to read and react to a very long, 25 pages or so, memorandum that I sent him that same month. I had outlined the vision I had for the University 101 course and the recommendations I would pursue to make the course fulfill its potential for really making a positive difference for students and the larger university. I had been warned by insiders who knew the new president well not to send him anything of any length as he would not read it! I disregarded the advice and received a reply that he not only had read it but found noteworthy several things I had written. He also added the admonition that I was never to write him at such length again!

The other and far more important thing President Patterson did was to make a decision as to how the University 101 program was to be evaluated and by whom. First the latter: In order to ensure objectivity and credibility, it was decided that I, as the program administrator, was *not* to be responsible for the evaluation. Instead, one of the most important decisions of the 50-year history of University 101 was to assign this to Paul P. Fidler, an assistant vice president of student affairs and tenured associate professor of higher education. Fidler was held in high esteem by all who knew him as a very wise, low-key, modest, highly principled, fair, and logical thinker and evaluator. Everything about him suggested credibility. In retrospect I think what he was about to do is the single most important variable to explain why we still have University 101 today in its 50th year. What then was his plan for evaluating University 101? This was important for us at USC, of course, but this also became *the* model for future assessment of hundreds of other first-year seminars.

First, he would review the entire background leading up to the adoption of the University 101 course, including a review of Faculty Senate minutes pertaining to the debate for its authorization. And, of course, this would also include the specifics of the adopted course description. Those of most consequence were the following: The course *was not* required; it was to be an elective open to all first-year students. Secondly, it was to be a three-credit course. And thirdly, the course was to be pass/fail graded. Fifty years later the course is still an elective, still three credits, but is letter graded.

The next step was to survey and interview all the people who actually taught University 101 in its first three fall terms, 1972–1975, to ascertain their explicit goals and objectives and to determine how these were communicated to the students in the official syllabi created by the course instructors. Note that there was not an official, one-size-fits-all uniform course syllabus. Instead, we had told instructors that this was to be "the course you had always wanted to teach but had never before had the opportunity to do so." In other words, a high value was assigned to instructor academic freedom. The faculty were also surveyed as to their self-assessment of what they thought was accomplished in their section of University 101. In addition, Fidler wanted to ascertain what first-year students and their families had been told during preterm orientation—what this course was to be about and why students should consider taking it. Fidler was very aware of the research on the impact of expectations on student outcomes, and he was trying to fathom the expectations that were being set for our students about what to expect from University 101 and its benefits.

Fidler also wanted to know what University 101 students actually did in or associated with this course and how University 101 students performed academically during their first semester in class compared to non-University 101 students. To get at this he designed what came to be called "The Freshman Survey." This was to be administered to essentially a captive audience of first-year students in their required English 101 course. He also decided not to tell the students that the purpose of this survey was to evaluate the University 101 course so as to avoid any possibility of what he called the "halo effect." Instead, the students were told the survey was an attempt to ascertain what they had experienced during their first term of college. However, in the student demographic section students were asked, "Did you take University 101?" Student responses to this one question enabled subsequent analyses to be conducted as to the similarities/differences of what University 101 participants versus nonparticipants actually did in the first term of college and how they felt about their overall college experience.

Specifically, students were asked to rate their knowledge and awareness of a set of university resources and services. Then the students were asked whether they had actually sought assistance from such services. Students were also asked about the extent to which they had participated in extracurricular activities. They were also queried about their out-of-class interactional patterns with faculty and staff, and they were asked about their attendance patterns in out-of-class activities such as attending plays, concerts, speakers, and so forth. They were asked to self-evaluate their levels of satisfaction with respect to the overall quality of the orientation they had received to the university.

Another extremely important component of the evaluation was for the university to do something it had never done before—namely to create special data files for analysis of student retention rates as measured for students' who had entered the university and were returning for the fall semester of 1975. An important differentiation was made of all students' predicted grade point average (PGPA) that had been generated for each new student during the admissions process based on their high school rank in class combined with scores on required standardized aptitude tests (e.g., SAT). That PGPA was to be compared to the actual GPAs earned by both the experimental and control groups in their first term. Demographic characteristics of all students, both the University 101 and nonparticipating student cohort, were analyzed on a disaggregated basis as a function of race, gender, and ethnicity. Once these retention findings were disseminated and considered, they really took over the narrative about the impact of the course. Specifically, his findings were the following:

- *Retention differences.* Most notably, the experimental group, the University 101 participants, had a higher retention rate than the non-University 101 control group in spite of the fact that the University 101 students had a *lower* predicted GPA than the nonparticipants. In other words, those students who, the data predicted, would have lower retention rates actually were retained at a higher level. What might explain this?
- *Knowledge and use of university services.* We found that University 101 students had a higher reported knowledge level of the university's services and resources than students who had not taken the course. But, what about use of those services? We also found that University 101 students reported higher usage levels of helping resources and services.
- *Out-of-class interaction and joining.* We found that University 101 students were more likely to interact with faculty outside of class. They also reported higher levels of group-joining behaviors and more frequent attendance at plays, concerts, lectures, and so forth.

- *Overall satisfaction with orientation quality.* What about overall levels of satisfaction about the quality of orientation provided by the university to its new students? Once again, University 101 students reported a higher level of satisfaction with orientation.
- *Special effect on African American students.* Another important finding initially, and over time to the present, was that the cohort of students who seemed to gain the most from course participation as compared to those who did not were first-year Black students. In another important study circa 1986 looking at the characteristics of USC African American graduates when compared with Black nongraduates, the finding was that Black students who had taken University 101 in their first year of college graduated at a higher rate than Black students who had not taken University 101. The research also found that Black students who graduated had been more likely to have had a fellow Black roommate in the first year. Now that was a finding that really grabbed my attention given my own experience as an undergraduate having to go see the president of my college to demand the right to live with a Black student.

One possible explanation for these differences might be the fact that the course was never required. Hence these students had chosen and entered this course voluntarily. It could, therefore, be hypothesized that volunteers would engage in a more positive manner than those who had not volunteered. To pursue this possible line of explanation, we explored with students the reasons they had decided to take this course. Many cited the fact that the course was promoted in orientation. Others reported that the university had sent information to their home address recommending participation in University 101 and that their parents had seen such communication. Some students put it more bluntly: "My parents told me I had to take this course!"

Further, to explore this "volunteer syndrome" hypothesis, Fidler analyzed data from the university's first-year student responses to the Cooperative Institutional Research Program's (CIRP) annual freshman survey, which measures levels of high school student participation in cocurricular activities. For our population, no significant differences were found in high school participation patterns in University 101 versus non-University 101 students that would explain why some of these students were more likely to take this course than others. Another hypothesis that emerged was the effect of academic advisors advising some students, but not others, to take this course.

The most significant result of Fidler's research was to persuade the university president, William H. Patterson, to issue a brief statement on the results of the evaluation along with his decision that "University 101 would continue as long as there was student and faculty interest." And here we are, 50 years later. Thank you, Paul Fidler and President Patterson!

For chapter discussion questions, click the link or scan the QR code to visit Appendix C of the Online Compendium.

https://styluspub.presswarehouse.com/uploads/5e35cd13add3605ede5537f
a2a5159aac11d5b57.pdf

9

EVOLUTION OF
UNIVERSITY 101

Major Developments and Research Outcomes

After the initial studies, University 101 continued to be a laboratory for research on college students. In 1987, a doctoral student, Mark Shanley, who was a senior student affairs officer, proposed to me a dissertation topic that would attempt to measure whether the first-year retention rates in favor of University 101 students would hold up through graduation. Initially, I was very nervous about pursuing this as I did not want to be held accountable for first-year-through-graduation persistence. I was happy to have responsibility for first-to-second-year retention, but there were so many other factors, experiences, and individuals involved in student success after the first year that initially I did not want to pursue this question. However, I soon came to my senses, and I decided to support Shanley's dissertation research. I concluded if we/I were really doing a good job of getting students started out well in college then we should expect higher graduation rates. And I definitely wanted to know the long-term reality of what we were or were not accomplishing. The findings over three consecutive entering student cohorts were that University 101 students had an overall aggregate higher graduation rate of about 5%. Now this was real confirmation of lasting impact from our efforts in helping students start out successfully in college. And I am proud to know and report that the higher graduation rates of the University 101 participants has been another consistent tradition of the course for 50 years.

Another narrower, but still important study we did on the impact of University 101 was conducted in the 1980s after the discovery of the AIDS virus and the resulting intervention we developed for students taking University 101 entitled "Sex and the College Student." This intervention was a partnership effort involving the Division of Student Affairs, the student health center, the USC School of Public Health, and the USC Medical School. We developed this initiative because we wanted to provide our students protection from AIDS and other sexually transmitted diseases. Many of our in-state students had experienced little to no sex education in the state's public schools, which were the primary source of new students for USC. The initiative featured group presentations by the charismatic, provocative, and popular university chief student health center physician, Dr. James Turner. Turner's presentations were coupled with small group discussions for all University 101 students. This particular study looked at the correlation between students' sexual decision-making patterns and their participation in University 101. Once again, different behavioral choices for University 101 students were documented with the finding that University 101 participants, especially females, were more likely to take responsibility for safer sexual decisions than were non-University 101 participants— decisions that could prolong their lives and prevent unwanted pregnancies.

Unquestionably, it was the findings related to retention that were most significant both to USC and the wider higher education community. To remind readers, while increasing student retention is a high priority institutional goal today for many colleges and universities, the desire and intent to accomplish increased retention had never been put forward as a rationale and goal for creating the University 101 course. This outcome then was quite serendipitous, but hugely profound. Once this was established, it became and still is a powerful driver for support of this course concept. But what mattered most was the recognition of the experiences, activities, and information we could intentionally provide for new students that would enhance their retention. This retention finding was so compelling, however, that the university provost, Keith Davis, gave me a directive in 1976 to "go out and sell it." And by this he meant he wanted me to be assertive about writing, speaking, and consulting externally about our University 101 model.

We had some other big take-aways from this pathfinding research. We learned that another key element of the "secret sauce" was delivering University 101 (and ultimately other student success initiatives) through an intentional structure and process for an operational partnership involving faculty, academic administrators, and student affairs professionals.

The second was that what we now call "assessment" really mattered only if you actually did something with the assessment findings, translating them into action that would lead to educational decision-making for improvement purposes. A corollary of this was the need for educational leaders to be explicit as to how specific assessment findings led to specific decisions and improvements. That became the essential ingredient to the University 101 success story.

Therefore, for the next nearly quarter century I would constantly tell any college and university internal and/or external audience I spoke to that I believed the most important reason University 101 was still going strong was because of the widespread awareness of our assessment findings. Awareness of the findings was coupled with the continued pursuit of ongoing assessment and use of the assessment results to make decisions for improvements. Thus, University 101 became in itself a gold standard for independent, objective, professionally delivered assessment. An essential part of this model was having this done *not* by yours truly but by independent researchers external to the University 101 program.

On this journey University 101 became a popular vehicle and context for university faculty to conduct research on human subjects. For example, one investigation by professor of psychology, Tom Cafferty, revolved around what in the discipline of psychology was known as attachment theory. In this line of investigation, it was realized that University 101 was really a vehicle for the intentional development of "attachment" between new students and other individuals within the university and with the university itself.

In 1999, three researchers at USC investigated the impact of participation in the University 101 faculty training workshop on teaching practices across the curriculum. They found that workshop participants did transfer a number of skills and activities learned in the workshop to their discipline-based teaching.

The course today is led by a unique individual, our fourth leader in 50 years, Dan Friedman, who is not only an expert administrator and designer of a first-year seminar, but also an expert on assessing the outcomes of such an intervention. In conclusion, on the matter of assessment, I want to recognize the seminal accomplishments in assessment of my beloved, late colleague, Paul P. Fidler. I can summarize my focus here on the importance of assessment by saying no assessment, no sustainability of University 101.

The Evolution of University 101: Major Developments

I would not have you think that once we started our Freshman Year Experience Conference series in 1982 that all attention to our course, University 101, went out the window. To the contrary, course enrollments continued to grow. And in this regard, I consistently resisted any pressure to move the course away from its voluntary status to being a required course. My thinking was this: If the desire is to impact all students you don't technically have to require all of them to do something. This is because of a concept we call "critical mass," which very simply means once you get a sufficiently large proportion of any total population engaging in some behavior or practice, by implication you have some influence over the entire group (e.g., achieving herd immunity through vaccination). To wit, in University 101 we consistently reached 80% of the entering class. And all of those students had friends, roommates, siblings, and ultimately their own children attending the university. If two students share a room, and one takes University 101 and learns in the course how to use the university library, that student can share this useful skill with the other student. Similarly, if you can influence, through University 101, one student to practice safe sex decisions, that student's partner is influenced also by that experience. An additional part of my rationale not to pursue required course status was to avoid any perception that I was trying to build an "empire" by stealing full-time-equivalent students that other units might lose if students took my course instead. I believed then, and do to this day, that bigger is not always better, another belief that differentiates me from some other leaders. The course then has remained highly effective to the present while being a voluntary (elective) choice. Another major course component we have not changed is the number of credit hours the course carries. The three hours of credit is a huge motivator and reward and gives University 101 both the appearance and substance of a "real" college course.

Changing the Type of Grading

When the course was established in 1972 it was designed as a pass/fail (P/F) course. The rationale in that era of "make love not war" was that we needed to try to motivate students to learn how to take positive advantage of the University for intrinsic reasons. It was also the thinking of the original designers that the course would be more effective if traditional grade pressures were eliminated altogether through the awarding of pass/fail. However, the students didn't see it that way. For years we received student complaints about the amount of work they were being required to do vis-à-vis the type of grade they were eligible to receive. They told us the P/F grading was actually a disincentive to really invest in the course. And thus, the course had not been a model for a real college course. This was exactly the opposite of the original outcome we had sought. The instructional faculty and staff agreed. They had been telling me for years that they would also take the course more seriously if they could award letter grades. Admittedly, I had been nervous about even attempting to change the grading structure because to do so would have meant we had to seek approval from the University Committee on Curricula and Courses and then the Faculty Senate. I truly knew how the system worked and had not wanted to open what I feared could have become a Pandora's box on unknown consequences and revisions that I had not requested and would not like. But eventually, I decided it was time to set aside my fears of this governance review and do what was right for students. I submitted the change, and it was approved with only brief discussion in the Faculty Senate.

Peer Leaders

The other game changer was to bring to USC an innovation seen elsewhere. This was the practice of utilizing peer leaders, meaning the pairing of the University 101 full-time instructor (faculty or staff member) with a qualified and properly prepared undergraduate or graduate student leader. I had seen this development at multiple institutions such as Baldwin Wallace College (now University) in Ohio and Kean College (now University) of New Jersey and was intrigued by its possibilities for University 101. I was well aware of a line of research-based thinking that had long reported the greatest influence on decision-making by undergraduate students as being the influence of their fellow students. I decided that the lowest risk approach to this change was for me to pilot this program in one section with myself as the instructor of record. I picked as a teaching partner one of my former University 101 students, Lisa Huttinger. Together we planned the course, every aspect of it, with Lisa providing input to me on the design of the syllabus, construction and grading of tests/papers, and cofacilitation of all classroom activities. Personally, I loved teaching with Huttinger and was impressed with our students' response to her. She actually enabled my well-intentioned wisdom to be received more willingly by students than if I had been teaching alone. Huttinger could also be the bad cop in ways that I could not, and she could go into residence halls to track down absent students in ways that I could not possibly have considered doing. I also found her to be a tougher grader than me. After one semester of this arrangement I was sold. I asked my codirector of University 101, Professor Dan Berman, to develop a full-fledged peer leader process. And what he did was amazing and is flourishing today, thanks again to Berman and his successor, Dan Friedman.

Basically, the design is this: We mount, each year, a competitive application process for being a peer leader. The student must be nominated, and only students with a 3.0 or better GPA may be considered. The peer leaders must go through a training workshop just like their instructor partners. But, in addition, the peer leaders must enroll in a graded, three credit, graduate-level education course titled "The Teacher as Manager." This course becomes the instructional vehicle in which we develop an even higher skill level in already high-achieving students and for which the coteaching of University 101 is the mandatory lab requirement. Our belief here is that all graduates will ultimately be leading in some kind of human organization and that an essential skill of all leaders is the ability to teach. The University 101 course structure became a learning experience to empower both entering students and our most promising upper-division students to give us another crack at shaping the values and behaviors of our students. As one of my peer leaders put it: "I am much more particular about what I do out in public because I would not want any of my University 101 students to see me setting a bad example for them!"

Becoming a Faculty/Academic Administrative Leader

While I am most likely to describe my fundamental role in higher education as being that of a faculty member, I still have to acknowledge my role as an academic administrator. But I think it was my ability to combine the skills, roles, and identities of both faculty member and administrator that enabled my success. I first had to learn to be a faculty member—I had had no training as such. I also had to learn to be an administrator, and I had had no training for that either.

What I knew and had learned about being a teaching faculty member I learned from my faculty models in undergraduate school (hardly any in graduate school) and from the developmental experiences I had, especially in my early years, 1967–1975, at USC. I drew on what I learned from my teaching in one of USC's open-access commuter two-year colleges, from my teaching of military students, from teaching women students in a single-gender institution, and from my teaching of economically disadvantaged students (and even living with them) in Upward Bound. I drew on my experimentation with video-based teaching and correspondence courses and finally from the University 101 faculty development workshop—the first one I attended at President Jones's invitation, and then the workshops I personally facilitated each year thereafter for 25 years.

My abilities as a teaching faculty member were recognized early in my career, in 1975, when I was selected to receive the Amoco Outstanding Teaching Award, the university's highest award for teaching excellence. This came at the end of my fifth year as a full-time faculty member and before I had earned tenure. I was awarded tenure and promotion to associate professor in 1977, after my fourth year as assistant professor. Four years later in 1981 I was promoted to full professor and was told I was the youngest "full" at the university at only age 36.

During this same period, I had learned the importance of extensive faculty service on university committees. In my earliest years of committee service, I was usually the most junior faculty member on the committee and hence very often was made the secretary. When that happened, I resolved to show my more senior faculty colleagues the best committee minutes they had ever seen. In part that contributed to my being elected by the university faculty-at-large as university faculty secretary, of both the entire faculty and the Faculty Senate. I served in this role for 3 years from 1980–1983 and resolved to be the best faculty secretary they ever had. My minutes were so incredibly complete I became a legend in my own time for an academic document genre that most faculty and academic administrators had never even paid any attention to before. But my minutes were read and often quoted, sometimes making people happy or unhappy.

During this same period, from 1974–1981, I had to learn to become an administrator. There were no professional development activities provided for such. Therefore, I sought out a number of administrative leaders that I could learn from and be tutored by, especially my own dean, a recovering former All American football player and football coach and some kind and patient administrators in the Office of Budget and Finance, who taught me about university fiscal management. During this period, I had two enduring accomplishments:

- I created and led, with three other colleagues, the university's first-ever new faculty and executive staff orientation, conducted every fall for a number of years.
- I became chair of a special subcommittee to study the structure of the university's summer school operations, which led to significant restructuring of those.

I was growing up as a university professor and learning how to teach, serve, lead, and administer. These endeavors were preparing me for the answers to the question "What do I do for the rest of my academic life now that I have become a full professor in a major research university—the best gig in America?"

During this period, I was developing an unwavering loyalty to the university and the people of South Carolina, so much so that by the time I reached full professor rank, combined with this tremendously gratifying work with University 101, I would never consider working for any other institution. That conviction only became more pronounced as subsequent developments further heightened my commitment. I kept remembering my father's advice to me: "Son, find a good company and stick with it!" I had found my good company (both the organization and the people). The company was already very supportive of me and was giving me one opportunity after another. That was to continue for another 20 years. I can accurately say that I was never denied anything I asked for in terms of something I wanted to do or lead.

What I was also learning during this period was how faculty think, work, create, discover, and find the very best possible ways to make use of the extraordinary freedom the profession gives us. This has yielded a bias of mine whereby I believe that if you haven't come up through the faculty leadership ranks, you are somehow at a disadvantage in student success work, given the outsized influence the faculty culture has on everything we do in the academy. And to really understand and work within that culture, I fundamentally believe the best preparation to do so is to have been, or still be, "faculty" in your thinking about the academy.

For chapter discussion questions, click the link or scan the QR code to visit Appendix C of the Online Compendium.

https://styluspub.presswarehouse.com/uploads/5e35cd13add3605ede5537f a2a5159aac11d5b57.pdf

IO

THE CONFERENCES
ON THE FRESHMAN
YEAR EXPERIENCE AND
A TRANSFORMATIVE
NATIONAL MOVEMENT

The First-Year Experience

W hat in a traditional faculty career (actually, mine was never "traditional") does a faculty person do after reaching the apex of the career ladder in terms of institutional designation of rank, the full professorship? In other words, "OK, John, you are 36 years old; now you are supposed to be all grown up; what are you going to do for the rest of your life?" One colleague, a PhD-level, full-time counselor in the university's counseling center suggested to me an answer: "John, all you have to do now is come into the office, turn off the lights, and go to sleep!"

The notion that full professors are less "productive" than junior faculty is one promoted by some critics of the tenure and ranking system. While I will admit I have known some full professors who seem to be coasting, most of those I have known don't pull back at all, and to the contrary, go on to even further levels of depth in and engagement with their discipline and specialized body of work, whatever that is. They are lifelong learners, discoverers, seekers, critics, researchers, and scholars. Those faculty were my aspiration. The traditional measure of productivity, of course, is publication. And with that measure alone I have been far more productive as a full professor than as an assistant or associate professor. For example, I have written eight books later in my career versus one book early in my career before full-professor status.

This meant that my focus as a unique kind of activist scholar, one whose research produces some type of tangible societal outcome(s), had become the first-year higher education experience. Not only was my focus on the characteristics of first-year students, but also on what they actually do in their first year. Even more importantly, my interest was on what do college and university educators actually do and provide for beginning college students. My challenge was then how to direct and expand this research focus as a faculty member so that I could learn and disseminate more about the first year than I had been able to do up to the point of my promotion. I was looking then for a win/win strategic focus and practice. Yes, selfishly, I would gain by achieving my scholarly objectives, but surely my university and the larger higher education community would benefit as well, and even more so than I would individually.

As context, in 1981, I had been the director of University 101 for 7 years, during which time I had earned tenure and two faculty promotions. I had played a leading role in exporting the University 101 concept to a growing number of other institutions. However, there was no single, unique higher education academic conference focused on the understanding and responding to the needs of first-year students. Nor was there any professional association for individual educators or institutions that focused on first-year students and their success in the first year of college. And there was no journal or publication series focusing on this topic. In other words, the study of the first year of college was not a bona fide discipline or body of knowledge. How could I change that? How could I transform our work on the first year of college to those kinds of professional and scholarly outcomes? At this point of contemplation about my future with this work, in retrospect, I guess this was my version of the 7-year itch. Should I stay with this work or move on to something else? Given my loyalty oath to the late President Jones, in some ways the "something else" wasn't an option. What I really wanted to do was something, anything, from which I could learn more about leading and developing such courses to teach students how to be successful in college and from which many others could learn too.

The Roller Bag Moment

What happened next I like to refer to as my "roller bag" moment. Think of something that has been created, generally something that represents an improvement over the status quo. And that something has become relatively ubiquitous. Whatever it is, it has attracted numerous adherents and users.

A good example is the roller bag. Can you remember going on trips lugging suitcases by lifting them and carrying their full weight with one of your arms? Can you remember these heavy bags when straps were finally added so that you could sling the strap over a shoulder and walk leaning to one side like you were a sail blowing in the wind? Roller bags have been a back savior for me. Not only do I have roller bag–style luggage, I also have a roller bag briefcase. I also see roller bag-like backpacks and bookbags that no longer have to be carried on your back like you are a beast of labor. Now all you have to do is pull the thing behind you. Things have gotten even better in the past several years as the devices have moved from two to four wheels, known as "spinners," making their ease of mobility even greater. Personally, I can't imagine what traveling would be like without roller bag luggage.

Where am I going with this? The so-called "First-Year Experience" became my roller bag moment. I invented a concept that many others could have invented, but just hadn't done so—yet. I recognized a need, actually multiple needs, that had been around for some time, but no one had acted on them or created a response in the academic marketplace to address a particular set of needs. The need was for a specific product of sorts, and a process, something that people could do, use, adapt to suit their own institutional and individual needs.

What were those needs that I had been observing and finally decided to do something about?

- If you were a college or university educator and wanted to learn more about improving the success of first-year college students, there were no conferences other than an annual meeting provided by the National Orientation Directors Association. That meeting focused, as its title implied, on collegiate orientation as delivered by student affairs professionals and students. There was no conference looking at the academic experience of students in the first year, how to teach them the skills and behaviors of college success, and how to do so using a curricular vehicle known as the first-year seminar.
- There was no convening designed to bring together in one experience three cohorts of college educators—faculty, academic administrators, and student affairs professionals—all focused on the common topic of how to improve the success of new students.
- There was no developed philosophy that might offer to educators a shared vision or set of aspirations to improve the first year of college.
- There was no literature base to articulate a vision for how to improve the first year or to report results of research on students or improvement efforts.

These needs had coalesced for me at the same time I was promoted to full professor. Also, after 7 years of leading a first-year seminar, I was realizing just how great the unmet needs of first-year students were, especially those who were not children of privilege as I had been.

Launching the First Conference on The Freshman Year Experience

My roller bag moment was a decision that became transformative. In the fall of 1981, after my promotion, I decided to try to establish a conference to bring together higher education faculty and staff who wanted to increase the success of new students. The need for such a gathering had been there for some time, especially since 1965 and the momentous Higher Education Act, which made it possible for millions of students for whom college was never designed to come to college for the promise of greater opportunity and upward social mobility.

What did I know about organizing a conference? Absolutely nothing! But that didn't stop me. I knew I could learn. Where would I get whatever money was needed to launch such an endeavor, and whom could I get to assist me? What would the essential features of the conference be to ensure initial success, and where could I do this that would make delivery easier and keep costs lower? There was one obvious answer for me: USC!

The components of my original vision for this conference were the following:

- This would be an academic conference where people would present papers and deliver presentations. And they would pay the university a modest fee for that privilege and pleasure.
- It would also be a social gathering for networking and socializing to create relationships as a basis for future collaborative work.
- We would attempt to build a big tent that would be open to a wide cross section of higher education professionals: faculty, academic administrators, and student affairs staff members.
- As an enticement to address multiple motivations for educational travel, we would host this event during a time of year when many Americans wanted a break from their winter experience: February.
- We would pick a city with reasonably priced accommodations and a relatively warm climate for a February convening: Columbia, South Carolina. People could come to Columbia, escape the northern snows, play some golf for which South Carolina was famous, and satisfy their curiosity about South Carolinians.

- We would host the meeting on the USC campus in addition to using commercial conference hotel space.
- We would try at the very beginning to get educators from Canada. I had already been interacting with a number of Canadian institutions about the University 101 concept and therefore had a developing network in Canada dating back to 1978.
- We would keep administrative costs low. I had one administrative assistant and believed that she and I could do anything that needed to be done. I will be forever thankful to her, Vicky P. Howell, who ended up making a university career out of doing this kind of work with me for 20 good years.
- We would utilize the university's hospitality management degree program, which had knowledgeable faculty and student graduates who could help us think through how to organize such an event. In that regard, one of my former students who respected me had graduated and become the meetings sales manager for the downtown Holiday Inn, which was surrounded by the university. Normally, if someone walks in off the street wanting to book meeting space and order hotel catering, there are requirements such as credit verifications, contracts, and up-front deposits. I didn't have any of that. But what I had was the willingness of this former student to book my event in her Holiday Inn with no credit check, no deposit, and just her confidence, inspired by her former experience with me as one of her professors, that we would make a success of this.

We marketed the conference in the fall of 1981, using very inexpensive "Ditto machine" marketing flyers. We mailed these using bulk mail to U.S. and Canadian higher education administrators and faculty. I solicited a number of proposals for session topics and presenters, but many proposals came in from individuals with whom I had never interacted.

I can't believe, in retrospect, that I used a ridiculously lengthy and uninspiring name for an inaugural meeting: "A National Conference on the Freshman Seminar/Freshman Orientation Course Concept!" My attendance goal was 50. I thought if I could get 50 people to come to unknown Columbia that I would learn and so would they. But to our great surprise, 173 individuals registered. This was a huge wake-up call for me. It told me there really was a market for my particular roller bag. And who were these 173? Exactly those to whom we had marketed: academic and student affairs administrators and faculty, all with one thing in common—an interest in first-year students. To our delight, this was not just a U.S. phenomenon; there was a small but engaged cohort of Canadian snowbird educators, exactly as I had hoped, confirming my hunch that interest in this new work was reaching beyond U.S. borders.

What resulted from this convening? The concluding session of this first conference was entitled "Where Do We Go From Here?" This was February 1982. I was the session facilitator, and the attendees gave me a vision for the rest of my career. They told us the following:

- Do another conference, John.
- Do it in Columbia. We loved everything about being here: yes, the climate, the people, the manageability of a small city like Columbia, and the beautiful, historic USC campus.
- But change the name and the focus to something shorter and more inviting. Not all of us have a first-year seminar. But we all have first-year students. Move the focus beyond just first-year seminars to other ways we are helping first-year students.
- Keep inviting non-U.S. educators. What you started as a U.S. activity could and should become an international movement to improve the beginning college/university experience.

And this is exactly what we did. Thankfully, I was given constructive feedback from some of my USC colleagues who told me that the actual meeting content had been great, but some of the administrative aspects of the conference had been a bit rough. Two very able colleagues then volunteered to help organize the second conference: Barbara Alley and Mary Stuart Hunter. "Stuart" ultimately became the principal conference organizer and director, a role she occupied from 1983 until 2018. Much of the ensuing impact of these conferences was due to Stuart's organizational abilities and commitment to the cause.

I gave alternative conference names a great deal of thought and centered on the following rationale. What if we focused the next conference not on these courses to help first-year students but on these four themes:

- Who are our first-year students, and what do they need to be more successful?
- What are institutions actually doing—and/or not doing to increase the success of first-year students?

- Who are the educators with ideas and a vision for improving the success of all beginning college students?
- What might be a common rationale for why the first year matters that we could pursue?

The title we selected for the second conference was simply "The Freshman Year Experience" (FYE). The basic idea was that most beginning college students have something equivalent to a year, at least in terms of required credits, and it is an "experience" of some sort. In our marketing for this second conference, we focused broadly on the entirety of the beginning college experience. We did so by inviting people to come join a dialogue to pursue such questions as these:

- Do your students have a freshman year experience?
- Do your students need a freshman year experience?
- If so, just what might that freshman year experience consist of, and who would provide this?
- What kinds of freshman year experiences are being offered by different colleges and universities?

A principal advantage of the new title was that it was succinct. It could be remembered and easily quoted. And it came to be just that. And it is still being widely used all over the world.

The response going forward was amazing:

- founding year, February 1982: 173 attendees
- 1983: 351 attendees
- 1984: 500 attendees
- 1985: First Canadian/American conference in Toronto
- 1986: FYE East Conference in Columbia, 1000 attendees; FYE West Conference in Irvine, CA, 600 attendees
- 1986: First International Conference on The First-Year Experience, Newcastle Upon Tyne Polytechnic, UK
- 1998: Important milestone: We abandoned the term *Freshman Year Experience* and moved to the gender-neutral *First-Year Experience*; this change was met with general, but not total, approval of our constituents
- 2020: Washington DC—approximately 2,000 attendees, just before the pandemic hit in March 2020
- 2021, the 40th year: a virtual conference attended by approximately 1,400 educators during the COVID-19 pandemic
- 2022, the 41st year: back in person for about 1,000 educators and approximately 300 more virtually

From a Conference Series to a Widely Replicable Concept

Why in 4 years had U.S. higher education devoted new energy to the freshman year? Was it really a "new" effort or just old wine in new bottles? The "freshman year experience" concept had become synonymous in the minds of many educators with USC, established in 1801; the first-year seminar, University 101, created in 1972; and my reputation created at the University of South Carolina in the 1970s! The rise of this concept in part was explained by its timeliness in terms of concerns about U.S. demographic trends, declining numbers of high school graduates, increased institutional competition for new students, rising concerns about student retention, and increasing attention being paid to the quality of undergraduate education. But the popularity of the first-year experience concept itself was a factor of additional forces:

- the enjoyment and inspiration from the conferences themselves and the fact that these conferences ultimately were offered in many locations in addition to our founding, flagship location in Columbia (69 conferences in 9 years from 1990–1999) and could be accessed in a "city near you"
- the new partnerships that arose on campuses involving faculty, academic, and student affairs officers, and much more recently what have become known as "student success" educators
- the aggressive marketing and branding of the Freshman Year Experience concept by USC
- the very language used, "Freshman Year Experience," which was easily converted to an acronym; the concept was easily replicable and could be adapted and redefined, and because of its succinctness, it could be easily remembered

What Then Is The Freshman Year Experience?

In a legal and proprietary sense, "Freshman Year Experience" is a registered trademark (now in its replacement form, "First-Year Experience") owned by USC. As the mark is used in commerce, it is designed to protect the university's proprietary interest in the branding of its revenue-generating conferences and publications.

It is most commonly the name given by colleges and universities to a particular "program," innovation, or initiative for its first-year students. These programs may be offered to all new students or a smaller cohort as some kind of boutique initiative.

The first-year experience can consist of multiple first-year experiences in the same institution but offered for different subpopulations. These can include developmental (nonmatriculated), matriculated, English as a second language, dual credit/concurrent enrollment, readmit, advanced placement, part-time, full-time, residential, commuter, first-time-in-college (FTIC), nontraditional, and/or transfer students.

Most importantly I argued that the freshman year experience meant a belief system, comprised of a set of values and producing a philosophy, about the educational value and importance of the first year of college as a foundational experience of the entire undergraduate experience. This could all be reduced to a phrase: *The first year matters*. It is a philosophy arguing that for decades many freshmen have been taken for granted and must be taken more seriously. The need for such a philosophy had been driven as a matter of educational and social justice and as an outgrowth of the civil rights movement and the ending of de facto and de jure discrimination.

The first-year experience became a call for more attention and therefore resources directed to *all* first-year students. It was my belief that if resources were directed to all students, the underserved populations needing the most attention would finally get their due. In essence, I was saying that the first-year experience is about the entirety of the beginning college experience, not about any one subcomponent of that experience or any one initiative to improve it.

But here's the rub: What people saw me doing was somewhat different in emphasis from what I was saying and writing. They heard me preaching a philosophy and advocating a set of values, but what they observed me doing was leading a highly successful educational intervention at USC known as University 101. Hence, as the First-Year Experience concept proliferated, it became particularly associated with the practice of offering credit-bearing courses to teach college students how to do college with the goal of increasing their persistence to the second year and beyond.

A Vision for a New Center Focused on the First Year

After 4 years of hosting the FYE Conferences in the United States, we had become a de facto, unofficial, national, and international resource center and clearinghouse for information and inspiration for improving the first year. This led me to decide in 1986 to propose to the university administration, and in particular, my provost, Frank Borkowski, that the university formalize our status and development by elevating and reconstituting us as some kind of university center or institute.

I had also been inspired to move in this direction by a friendship that had morphed into a mentor/mentee relationship, this time with another faculty member, John Whiteley, of the University of California, Irvine. Whiteley was/ is approximately 4 years my senior, also a full professor, and an international leader in multiple fields. He has also spent almost an entire career, about 50 years, practicing another central character trait I possess: institutional loyalty to one university coupled with the pursuit of social justice.

In 1985, Whiteley gave me a vision for how I could convert our embryonic Freshman Year Experience series into something much more "university-like," sustainable, and impactful. Specifically, in a San Francisco bar, he sketched out for me on a cocktail napkin a design for what is now known as USC's National Resource Center for The First-Year Experience and Students in Transition. Foolishly, I did not save that cocktail napkin, but it became the mental vision for what I would present as a formal proposal to my university in 1986. It is important to note that Whiteley's original vision for such a center was that while it could and should continue organizing the conference series, it needed to do more. This proposed center needed to act in accordance with the realization that we could reach far more people each year through the currency of the academic realm: publishing. This should include the establishment of a refereed journal and a series of monographs, books, and other publications. Whiteley contributed some of his own work to comprise our center's first published monograph on the topic of moral and character development in college students. All of that vision has come to pass.

In 1986, I put through university channels a proposal to create a "center," based at USC, which was approved at all levels culminating with the board of trustees. The proposal was then was forwarded for review by the state's Commission for Higher Education, which, in turn, recommended the center for start-up 3-year funding grant support. The legislature did authorize that support, and effective July 1, 1987, the National Center for the Study of The Freshman Year Experience became operational with a $200,000 seed grant from the State of South Carolina. And as of this writing, an evolved version of this center has been thriving for about 35 years.

My first task was to appoint a codirector for the center, just as I had done for the University 101 course in the person of Professor A. Jerome Jewler, and as I had done in the role of codirector for conferences and administration in the person of Mary Stuart Hunter. The first codirector of the center was Ray Murphy, who had served as vice president for student affairs at Penn State University. Murphy got things moving for 2 years and then left two successors: Dorothy Fidler as codirector and her part-time doctoral student, Betsy Barefoot. Several years later for health reasons, Dorothy Fidler decided to switch roles with Betsy Barefoot, making Barefoot the codirector, and these two able women scholars and editors launched what became very rapidly a prolific publishing program that established, most notably, a highly respected refereed: *Journal of The Freshman Year Experience* (now the *Journal of The First-Year Experience and Students in Transition*). The journal is published twice a year and was accompanied by a newsletter published four times annually that is now available electronically as "e-source" and by a steady series of monographs on a wide variety of topics, all focusing on undergraduate transitions.

The design was for a comprehensive academic unit, with three codirectors reporting to the provost through me as the founding executive director. The unit consisted of the University 101 course and its faculty development programs, the FYE domestic and international conferences, and the National Center for the Study of The Freshman Year Experience as a publishing and scholarship dissemination component. That was the structural design until my retirement in 1999. Throughout my tenure as the unit senior administrator, I attribute the success of these activities to four factors: the extraordinary abilities of the three codirectors; the continuing accumulation of more and more impressive evidence of impact of University 101 as determined through the assessments conducted by Paul Fidler for approximately 25 years and now expanded greatly by the University 101 director, Dan Friedman; the support of the 7 consecutive extraordinarily collegial provosts who directed my work and every USC president from 1972 to the present; and the receptivity to our work by multiple constituencies: students, faculty, staff, administrators, and trustees in the USC system and, more broadly, national and international educators, national and international conference attendees, and subscribers to our publications.

For chapter discussion questions, click the link or scan the QR code to visit Appendix C of the Online Compendium.

https://styluspub.presswarehouse.com/uploads/5e35cd13add3605ede5537f
a2a5159aac11d5b57.pdf

II

OTHER CONTRIBUTING FACTORS TO THE NATIONAL AND INTERNATIONAL FIRST-YEAR EXPERIENCE MOVEMENT

This chapter describes some key manifestations of the First-Year Experience movement, such as replication of the University 101 course at hundreds of colleges and universities; proliferation of FYE conferences in the United States as a dissemination mechanism; internationalization to Canada and the UK; a national-use textbook for students; a breakthrough book for the higher education community; contributions of the student affairs profession; and contributions of the American Association for Higher Education. The chapter also addresses the expansion beyond the first year, first looking at the senior year experience and then expanding to "students in transition" more generally.

Replication of the University 101 Course at Hundreds of Colleges and Universities

In the United States we reached peak numbers of high school graduates circa 1981, and there was keen interest in retaining more students out of an ever-shrinking pool. While University 101 and my work was focused on advancing all students, there was, at the same time, a growing national concern about the poor success rates of Black students, an issue that University 101 had addressed successfully.

I wish I could say that it was the altruism of higher education professionals, their genuine desire to help students, and their commitment to social justice that would explain the First-Year Experience movement momentum. But it was the lure of revenue that really did it. Generating more revenue required improving retention. And the first year would become the overriding focus for doing so, then as now—only now with a much greater emphasis on equity outcomes, thank goodness.

Proliferation of FYE Conferences in the United States as a Dissemination Mechanism

In addition to the freshman year experience national conferences previously mentioned, we added regional conferences and a series of 2-day workshops that we hosted in 69 different cities from 1990 to 1999. We also launched in 1987 a series of "special focus" FYE conferences for small colleges, community colleges, and STEM programs as well as technology-focused and athletic programs. This enabled us to reach thousands of new participants each year. This ensured that some kind of First-Year Experience program or initiative would and did spring up on almost every campus in America.

Internationalization to Canada and the UK

Because we were a major U.S. institution with a wide range of global activities, and because I believed that university faculty must be global in their reach to other like-minded colleagues, we launched two lines of international work. The first was Canadian, a joint partnership with Jim Griffith of the University of Prince Edward Island for a series of residential faculty development workshops, beginning in 1983. We expanded that to host Canadian/American conferences in Toronto, Halifax, Victoria, and Vancouver. We also published, in 1997, a major monograph on the Canadian first-year experience. I also traveled across the country extensively; for example, in 1990 I visited multiple institutions in five provinces from eastern Canada in Ontario to British Columbia.

Our first effort to launch an international version of the FYE conference outside North America took place in 1986 at Newcastle upon Tyne Polytechnic in the UK. The outcome of this first international conference was a decision to hold a second one, also in Britain, the following summer in Southampton. We then hosted successive conferences in Reading, Cambridge, Warwick, York, Manchester, and Edinburgh with detours to Ireland and Denmark!

The international conference series continued through 2011, and, sadly, at least from my perspective, was discontinued by my successors because these events didn't generate enough profit. Thankfully, parallel efforts developed in other parts of the world to maintain this momentum. Most notably, an ad hoc group of European tertiary educators launched the annual European First-Year Experience Conference (EFYE) series. My colleague, Stuart Hunter, was also very instrumental in advising the development of a series of international first-year experience–focused Pacific Rim conferences in Australia. As a milestone of sorts in terms of our capturing international interest in our First-Year Experience concept, *The Times* of London reported on July 29, 1988, "The First-Year Experience is also an industry in which the University of South Carolina is the market leader."

A National-Use Textbook for Students Is Born

A major step in the institutionalization of the First-Year Experience concept was the creation of a textbook. USC faculty colleague, A. Jerome (Jerry) Jewler and I decided to write such a textbook to support University 101.

As I have related previously, the course, University 101, was born in 1972, and it did not have a textbook. These types of courses did not constitute what the publishers would have called a "list." But a book was needed because this was a course for three credits, and students needed to have a common required reading. By that time there was sufficient knowledge to comprise a textbook focused on college success strategies. Textbooks are important because they can lend order and structure to courses themselves, and the absence of any texts for this course type suggested that we had not yet really arrived as a bona fide instructional/curricular genre. We were not yet legitimate, established members of the higher education disciplinary club. In a course like this, a text would have been a valuable professional development tool for the course instructors who had never studied nor done graduate work in "college success."

Jewler provided the breakthrough we needed. He was a talented teacher of copywriting in advertising courses and had been successful in getting a book published for his course on creative advertising copywriting by Wadsworth Publishing Company. Wadsworth was not an East Coast publishing powerhouse but a smaller flexible company that was more willing to take risks. Jointly, Jewler and I decided that we should take our book idea to Wadsworth. We did, and they liked the idea and decided to take a leap of faith and create a new market. The resulting book, published in 1985 as *College Is Only the Beginning*, was wildly successful. The company published a second edition in 1987 and made the decision to create a much more robust full-color text with other bells and whistles to hit the market in 1992. Our editor titled this book *Your College Experience* but informally called it "the battleship" that was designed to "blow the competition out of the water!" It too sold well and is now in its 14th edition. Eventually, after Jewler's retirement, Betsy Barefoot joined as coauthor.

This textbook development process was important because it demonstrated a viable commercial market for such a textbook genre. Once *Your College Experience* was out, it came to the attention of other publishing houses and the college textbook industry more broadly, a highly imitative and competitive business sector. This meant that the textbook options exponentially increased and a whole new market for producing educational materials to support the adjustment of first-year college students had developed. USC's University 101 course had solidified its position as the gold standard for still another innovation in this new and developing field. Of course, since the mid-1980s this industry has realized major consolidation and challenges so that there are now only four major college textbook firms, three of them publishing in this field of "college success."

The Big Break in Publicity: A *Chronicle* Story

As many readers know, the most prestigious regular news publication about higher education is *The Chronicle of Higher Education*. We had previously attracted the attention of other press outlets, including *The New York Times*, and had drawn thousands of participants to our FYE conferences; however, *The Chronicle* did not cover us until October 7, 1987. And when they decided to cover us, they really did—a huge, multipage spread under the headline "South Carolina's Gardner: Self Appointed Spokesperson for the 'Largest Educational Minority'—Freshmen." That really said it all! While I cannot measure this in any way empirically, my sense at that time was the number of inquiries we received at our center for information, referrals, and so forth increased significantly, with more and more people telling me that they had read about our work in *The Chronicle*. I am so thankful to *The Chronicle* reporter, Elizabeth (Liz) Greene, for her investment in this story and her ability to persuade her editorial leaders to devote this much ink to the full nature of this national effort to improve the success of first-year students.

Another Big Step: A Breakthrough Book for the Higher Education Community

In the 1980s, one of the many contributions that converged to generate momentum for the freshman year experience was the publication of a book that became widely read, utilized by campuses and influential educators.

This work, *The Freshman Year Experience*, published in 1989, was influential partly because of the publisher. In that era the premiere publishing house for books for and by higher education administrators and leaders was Jossey-Bass. I became involved in this project through no initial effort of my own, rather, because of an invitation I received from M. Lee Upcraft of Penn State University. Lee was a highly esteemed writer in the student affairs profession, and his name as the first author guaranteed us an initial readership. The book reached a wide audience and was successful by the standards of the publisher in terms of sales. It also became the lead for a series of six more books that I would coauthor and publish with Jossey-Bass from 1998–2016.

While our conferences and our center's own publishing activities had helped us reach many thousands and in turn influenced practice, other widely received books about educational innovations were also instrumental in the dissemination of the concepts we were espousing for the improvement of higher education. I had come to believe that in this work of institutionalizing innovation, publishing is essential. This is a mainstay of my professional belief system and something I have practiced consistently from 1989–2022, with my latest coauthored work (with Michael J. Rosenberg of Penn State and Andrew K. Koch of the Gardner Institute), entitled *The Transfer Experience: A Handbook for Creating a More Equitable and Successful Postsecondary System*, published in early 2021 by Stylus.

Contributions of the Student Affairs Profession

While I cannot gauge this with any kind of data-driven accuracy, it was my sense that for at least 15 years from the mid-70s to around 1990, the original impetus to do first-year experience-like initiatives on many campuses came from student affairs professionals. They saw, most importantly, that this would be good for students and that it was a mechanism they could utilize in order to work much more closely with faculty to drive a more holistic approach to student learning. As time evolved, emphases shifted, and the principal drivers of first-year seminars and other initiatives involving academic credit-bearing experiences were chief academic officers, many of whom had been nudged by the consciences of their student affairs colleagues.

Contributions of the American Association for Higher Education

For about 25 years, from 1978–2007, my primary professional affiliation outside USC was with the American Association for Higher Education (AAHE). AAHE's annual conferences, under the leadership of Russ Edgerton, Lou

Albert, Ted Marchese, and Pat Hutchings, had a huge influence on my work for USC and on my career. This organization was unique in its broad focus on many components of innovation in undergraduate education, coupled with its membership, which represented all sectors of institutional types and all types of faculty and academic and student affairs professionals. These truly diverse cross-sector and role-spanning convenings provided a unique opportunity for me to learn from a more diverse spectrum of educators than I would be interacting regularly with on my own campus. AAHE had, in particular, special "caucuses" for women, Hispanics, and Blacks, and I attended caucus meetings of all three for years. The association also provided me with occasional opportunities for speaking to the membership about our work.

One AAHE influence, in particular, was the 1990 Stand and Deliver Faculty Salute to 100 faculty from around the country who had "stood and delivered" for their institutions. I was one of those selected for this honor, and I took from this a replicable concept that continues to this day. As a participant myself in the moving recognition/celebration process I realized the power of honoring others. I turned to my colleague and codirector for our National Resource Center for The Freshman Year Experience, Betsy Barefoot, to organize a similar recognition process for what we called "outstanding freshman advocates." We found a commercial sponsor to underwrite this process, and each year we invite every chief executive officer of every accredited institution in the United States to nominate one individual from the campus who most personifies what we mean by an "outstanding freshman advocate." We select 10 annually who are vetted in categories by institutional types. This annual process continues and has been exceptionally well received by honorees and their campuses alike.

We also encouraged institutions to create their own parallel process at the institutional level. We did this at USC to walk our national talk. Thank you AAHE for the inspiration! I would still be a member if AAHE hadn't ceased operation in 2006–2007. The former president of AAHE, Russ Edgerton, became one of my mentors and the prime mover for Betsy Barefoot and me to start our own national, nonprofit institute, a development I will relate later in this work. Thus, it suffices to say that the influence AAHE had on my work lasts to this very day.

A New Field of Research and Scholarly Publishing Is Born

To be credible, any important field within higher education has to have a solid research foundation. The field must draw not only advocates, spokespersons, and practitioners but especially scholars, researchers, and writers. The USC National Resource Center for The Freshman Year Experience definitely spawned this kind of development. It can no longer be said there is no literature base for the study of the first year and other student transitions as I discovered in 1981.

Creating a Common Message/Script

The combination of all of the factors internal and external to our work had contributed to larger efforts of the university to create what I call the "common message" or "common script." I believe the best functioning organizations provide all those being newly introduced to the organization, and also their continuing staff, a consistent set of messages around values and purpose that are repeated by many different individuals and forms of messaging. This becomes an organizational "script," a form of self-talk that then we have to walk. The common script centers us. Students and their families arriving at USC would hear this common script from multiple speakers and communications: what we advise students to do; what successful students here do; and what it is that we are going to do for you.

Moving From an Exclusive Focus on the First Year to Include Other StudentTransitions

From 1982–1998, there were a number of additional spinoffs from the original concept of the University 101 course. In addition to the FYE conferences, other new professional development concepts emerged.

As my work for USC was evolving in the 1980s with this focus on improving the first year of college, I found myself slowly moving to a focus on another critical transition in the undergraduate years, an equally important bookend to the first year: the last year of college up to graduation. This was an opportunity to invent and innovate again, and to create what became known in U.S. higher education as two distinct, but related concepts: the senior year experience and students in transition.

In interactions with hundreds of higher education professionals at our conference series, I would occasionally take notice of their expressed interest in another transition—the one prior to and upon graduation. I noticed a number of parallels to the conversations around the first year that went like this:

- Students are experiencing a critical stage and phase of undergraduate education and transition.
- In both cases many are leaving either the environment of home or college.

- Both transitions involve uncertainty about what lies ahead.
- Both transitions are stressful and anxiety provoking, for both students and their families.
- Students can and do drop out from both transitions—first year and senior year—and hence do not graduate from the institution in a pattern of appropriate progression.
- Both are transitions in which students make decisions that have much longer-lasting impact.
- Both transitions are key foci of institutional assessment efforts to learn about student characteristics upon arrival and their outcomes upon departure.
- Successful accomplishment of both transitions can be realized by learning, practicing, and mastering certain types of knowledge and skills.
- Students in both transitions need intervention, support, and inspiration from faculty and staff. Colleges and universities can support students in both these transitions, for example through uniquely focused transition courses: first-year seminars and capstone courses.
- Successful transition in the first year yields retention to the second year. Successful transition in the senior year leads to retention in the ranks of alma maters' satisfied alumni.
- Institutions often lack a coherent plan to make first-year students successful and even more likely do not have a comprehensive approach for senior student success.
- Students in both populations have been taken for granted in various ways. This is even more likely the case for senior students.

As I found myself thinking more and more about the symmetry—or lack of it—between these two transitions, I had two other powerful influences, one personal and one professional. First, the personal: My stepson, Wynn Corley, had started his first year at the university in the fall of 1986. This finally gave me the opportunity to see my own university through the eyes of one of my children. There is no experience quite like that one to make some of us who may have worked at the place for years as I had to see all kinds of things differently. Some of what I saw was that my son had received far more attention in a first-year program (named "Opportunity Scholars") than he had received in his senior year. And this young man was going to be on a 5-year plan as a gentleman-C student working toward a Bachelor of Arts in Interdisciplinary Studies (that degree program I wrote about many pages ago that I helped create back in 1972).

As my son moved through undergraduate school, I fell under the inspirational spell of a woman who had a deserved reputation for being one of the most accomplished leaders for innovation in undergraduate education, Betty Siegel, president of Kennesaw State University. I had been working with Siegel for 6 years to help her innovate in her presidency at Kennesaw, especially around the first year. She had encouraged Kennesaw State to create a University 101 course modeled on the one we had at USC and an accompanying faculty/staff development program. I made many visits to Kennesaw and came to know Siegel and her family very well. I discovered something she was doing that connected with my rising senior son at USC: Siegel as a college president herself was teaching a senior capstone seminar in which she was focusing on preparing soon-to-graduate students for the transition to life after college and doing so from her disciplinary perspective as a psychologist. I was really taken with this idea. It was an epiphany for me, a profound insight that I would move to action in four ways. I would organize a national conference; lay the groundwork for a new transition course at USC; start working on a textbook for college seniors; and begin another book for educators focused on improving the senior year transition.

The Senior Year Experience Conference Series

My first action was to entice Siegel and Kennesaw State University to cohost with USC a first-ever "National Conference on the Senior Year Experience." We held this in Atlanta in March of 1990 for about 200 educators. Siegel also invited a number of corporate leaders to speak at the conference to share with participants from the ranks of the academy the experiences, skills, and types of knowledge they wanted in the graduates they would be hiring in both for-profit and nonprofit settings. And "déjà vu all over again," as Yogi Berra once said, we had a reporter, Denise Magner, from *The Chronicle*, attend this conference and write a major story entitled "Many Colleges Design Courses and Programs to Prepare Seniors to Live in the 'Real World.'" We offered encores of this conference for three more years in 1991, 92, and 94.

A Course for USC Seniors: University 401

The USC senior transition course, University 401, would not have been possible without the support of a fellow professor at USC, Keith Davis, the chair of our highly regarded Department of Psychology. Davis had been my first provost from 1974–1978, and I had reported to him as coordinator and then director of University 101. Davis liked what he saw of the kinds of proposed experiences we were developing for departing students, and he agreed to house the course in his department as an experimental course, Psychology 399, Senior Capstone Experience, beginning in 1994. He actually taught a section of the course as I did for multiple years.

After making appropriate revisions and quietly building informal support for the course among USC faculty, we finally decided the course was ready for prime time, meaning it could be put before the Faculty Senate for formal authorization as a permanent course in the university curriculum. What we proposed specifically was variable credit elective, from one to three credits, to be determined by whatever department wanted to offer this course for its majors. The course was adopted by an amazing unanimous vote on April Fools' Day, 1998. It probably helped that the "god of boring speakers" was on the schedule that day, and after that man talked the senators into a stupor, they were just ready to dispense with all business as rapidly as possible. Hence, there was not even a word of discussion about Gardner's latest idea to help USC students in transition. Over the next 24 years, University 401 has flourished beyond my wildest hopes and dreams under the leadership of my successor, Dan Friedman, and it is one of my accomplishments at USC of which I am most proud.

What did we do for students in University 401? First, it was an opportunity for students to confess to us some of the things they had not done or done enough of in their undergraduate courses. They were still with us, so it wasn't too late. For instance, some students were coming to the realization that they had not written enough. Nor had they gotten enough opportunity to speak in class, do group project work, or lead groups. We drew heavily from research of a friend of mine, Philip Gardner, the founder of Michigan State University's Collegiate Employment Research Institute. Gardner's research investigated the knowledge, skills, and attitudes that hiring officers of for-profit and nonprofit organizations were looking for in college graduates. We adapted those findings to course content. For instance, students in the course conducted research on various occupations and employment trends using the career center library. They were required to do work shadowing and to write a major paper on their own career assessment and planning process. The class did a team project on some aspect of what the university was or was not doing for seniors and publicly presented their findings and recommendations to a live audience of influential university faculty, department chairs, and administrators whom students had selected for personal invitations and who actually attended, much to the affirmation of the students.

The class included an examination of personal finance issues. Recent USC graduates came to class and spoke about their transition experiences.

Local employers also visited class and talked about what they were seeking in graduates. Finally, we had each student prepare a portfolio to document the various milestones of their own undergraduate experience to demonstrate what they had done and learned in college and toward what ends. The portfolio products were presented publicly, and students invited their parents, friends, and even some of their faculty to attend. Believe it or not, this course generated the highest levels of student satisfaction and affirmation of any course I had taught in my 32 years at USC, including even in my beloved University 101.

Other Major Books With National Implications for Practice

Given all that we were learning about the needs of seniors for certain types of learning experiences before they left college, we had undertaken dissemination through a national conference series, a textbook for students (*Ready for the Real World*, published by Wadsworth Publishing in 1994) and a course for students University 401. All this had taken 8 years to develop from 1990–1998. And now we were ready for a major book for fellow higher education professionals.

Once again, I turned to Jossey-Bass with a book proposal that was accepted. And in 1998, our book, *The Senior Year Experience*, was published, authored by me and a coauthor, Gretchen Van der Veer. The subtitle of the book summarized in a phrase what we most wanted to accomplish successfully for seniors: "Reflection, Integration, Closure, and Transition."

- We wanted to encourage reflection on the totality of one's college experiences in both the curriculum and cocurriculum. We wanted students to ask themselves, "What did you learn and how? What can you now do as a result? If you changed, how did that happen and as a result of what influences?"
- We also wanted to encourage integration of all that students learned and did: "How did you make sense of your learnings, and how can you synthesize and explain them to others? How was your curriculum integrated? How do you now understand and practice the virtues of persons educated in the liberal arts?"
- We hoped to provide closure for students: "This has been one of the most important experiences of your life. What can you do at its conclusion to tie it all together and make sense of it? How can you appropriately recognize your accomplishments and make the best possible decisions for how you will move on?"

- Finally, we aimed to help students with the transition: "You are making one of life's most important transitions; leaving, finishing undergraduate school. What does it take to make this transition successfully? And going forward, what are the transitions you will need to make in work, relationships, and family?"

Moving Beyond Conferences on the Freshman and Senior Year Experience to Students in Transition

In recounting the evolution of the Senior Year Experience (SYE) conferences, I reported that we offered four of them from 1990–1994. While we found significant interest in our addition of the senior year as a focus, that is something different from being able to afford to do so. The higher education conference business is an expensive and competitive enterprise, and to offer any meeting is a costly undertaking. We found over 4 years that we were barely breaking even on the SYE conferences. Therefore, in 1994 I made the decision to continue calling attention to the senior year but to imbed that focus in a broader meeting on "students in transition." The plan was to solicit proposals on topics pertaining to four major undergraduate transitions: first year, sophomore year, transfer, and senior year. We knew we would draw more people interested in the first year, and, in effect they would underwrite the costs for those interested the other transitions. And that is exactly what has happened.

We launched the first Students in Transition (SIT) meeting in Dallas in 1995 with about 600 enthusiastic attendees. And we have offered at least one of these SIT meetings every year since. The language of "students in transition" has found its way into nomenclature for campus-based organizational structures and personnel positions through which support is offered for not just one but multiple student transition issues. To this day, an annual conference opportunity for discussion of the senior year is still available through this structure, and it is one that pays for itself.

It's All in a Name: Changing One Word and Causing a Firestorm

In 1998, I decided it was time for me to personally and professionally bite a bullet that evoked for some the perception of political correctness. We had begun by calling our core concept "The Freshman Year Experience," and we gave that name to a conference series and a blind refereed journal. But I was not living in a vacuum, and I knew that gradually the term *freshman* was becoming harder and harder to defend. First, for some time the majority of America's first-year students had been women, not men. In a similar manner, the majority of those teaching what used to be called "freshman seminars" were not men either, but highly dedicated women. Further, the United States was the only nation I could find where beginning higher education students were termed *freshmen*. Instead, the more common terminology was *first-year* or *first-years*.

I came to the conclusion that the continued use of the term *freshman* was no longer defensible or appropriate for a USC trademark, a conference series, publications, or any other public-facing branding. Hence, I sought the official permission of the university administration to change the descriptive language for our center, conferences, publications, electronic mailing lists, and trademark to *first-year*. This was readily granted by my provost, Jerry Odom. However, when we issued a public announcement about the name change, especially on our electronic mailing list, it kicked off a firestorm from those who were more traditional. We toughed it out and did not give in, and there has been no hint of our ever going back to *freshman*, thank goodness. Language really matters.

For chapter discussion questions, click the link or scan the QR code to visit Appendix C of the Online Compendium.

https://styluspub.presswarehouse.com/uploads/5e35cd13add3605ede5537f
a2a5159aac11d5b57.pdf

ANOTHER IMPORTANT TRANSITION

Moving the Annual FYE Conference (and Ultimately Its Founder) Out of South Carolina

In 1994 I saw the political pendulum beginning to shift in South Carolina, and I sadly foresaw that the South Carolina legislature was going to take provocative action that would lead to a NAACP boycott of South Carolina. Fearing and predicting this, I sought assistance from the USC Legal Department to renegotiate a contract to insert a clause in our contract with the Marriott Corporation allowing us to bail from the contract and be held harmless from resulting financial damages to the hotel if a national civil rights boycott was announced against South Carolina. Were that to happen there was no way I could, in good conscience, invite fellow higher education professionals from all over the country and outside the United States to come to South Carolina. Sadly, that is exactly what happened. The Republicans took over state government, put up a Confederate flag in front of the state house, and the NAACP announced its boycott. Much further down this road, it took the murder of nine Black South Carolinians in a Charleston church in 2015 to force the state to take down the flag. But in the meantime, we had yanked our annual FYE conference out of Columbia and have been holding it outside of South Carolina every year since 2000. I was, and still am, so regretful that the boycott made it necessary for us to move our conference out of South Carolina, but I supported the NAACP decision to take this strong protest action.

A Conversation That Changed My Life

In January of 1998 I was making a presentation in a conference session in Washington DC, and I noticed in my audience one of my mentors, Russ

Edgerton, the immediate prior chief executive officer of the AAHE, on whose board I had served, and who was now serving as the chief higher education grants program officer for The Pew Charitable Trusts. At the conclusion of my session, Edgerton approached me warmly and asked me if we could have a coffee. Of course, I agreed, and in the context of this conversation he posed this extraordinary question to me, one of a lifetime: "John, if you had 1 to 5 years, and $1 to $5 million to do anything you had always wanted to do to improve the first year in American higher education—but never before had either the time or the money—what would you do?"

Hard as this is to imagine for anyone who knows me, I was speechless, so Edgerton suggested that we meet again: "Well, John, why don't we get together again in several months and we will revisit this—and, John, why don't you bring Betsy Barefoot with you?" Of course, I accepted his charge to meet. Our ultimate answer to Edgerton was to lay the foundation of our work for the next chapter of our work life.

A Decision to Do Something I Had Never Thought I Would Do: Leave USC

For my readers who do not know me, I can assume that by the time you get to this point in this book, you assume that I spent my entire work career at USC. That was my assumption too until the late 1990s. By that time I was beyond my 30-year point of service (at which I had become eligible for full retirement with lifetime health insurance benefits) to the university and the people of South Carolina. As I will relate, I did eventually move on. I will refer to this departure point as "early nonretirement." One of the influencers was Edgerton's action previously described. After finishing the planning grant he awarded, he was willing to offer a grant to move the proposal that Betsy Barefoot and I had submitted to action. We did want to take advantage of this opportunity, but it wasn't as simple as that, as I shall explain.

As the decade of the '90s had progressed, I had become a "single" person again, and also a single parent. The younger of my two sons left for college in 1994, creating for me the proverbial empty nest. It would be accurate to say that up until the late '90s I was a pretty typical male professional, disproportionately focused on my career, not my personal life. By the middle '90s my close USC colleague, Betsy Barefoot, and I had developed an additional personal relationship, which was a very good thing, as she introduced me to options for life outside my career that I had not considered previously.

One of those was a pursuit of the arts as an active hobby, not as a performer, but as an enthusiastic audience member and supporter. One special place we explored was Brevard, North Carolina, a little town in the west-ern North Carolina mountains outside of Asheville. What attracted me to Brevard was first the 50-plus year old, nonprofit Brevard Music Center, a summer, residential, classical music training institution for about 450 gifted young musicians (of which I ultimately became the chair of the board of trustees). The town was also blessed to have a moderate climate; proximity to the Asheville Regional Airport; a small, private, liberal arts college, Brevard College; and a dynamic and truly amazingly "progressive" local, family-owned newspaper, which spoke volumes to us about the progressive values of the community.

Betsy and I decided to explore the possibility of buying a lot and building a home in Brevard, which, beginning in 1997, we did. Other circumstances converged to solidify my decision to retire from the university.

The first was a visit to my office from a long-time colleague, Dorothy Fidler. The purpose of her visit was to tell me she had decided to retire. When she announced this, I started to congratulate her, but she immediately inter-rupted me to tell me this really wasn't good news. Instead, it was because her husband, one of my closest friends and colleagues at USC, had been diagnosed with a terminal illness. This decision then was to enable them to spend more of their remaining time together. This moved me to question more seriously what I was going to do with my remaining time.

In the same time period, the South Carolina state legislature adopted a measure to place a Confederate battle flag on a flagpole literally at the foot of the steps leading up into the legislative chamber. This was a symbol, a meta-phor of the ending of what had been a progressive, Democrat-led 34-year evolution in South Carolina to have the state finally rejoin the nation. This coincided with the increasing polarization between the two national political parties. The message was clear: South Carolina was going to take a hard right turn, and I knew I wasn't going to be a fit with that. I began to sense that I had been in the state for its best years and that it wouldn't resume moving to the political center, let alone to the left, during my lifetime. In 1999, North Carolina was seeming to be much more moderate in terms of public policy, including investment in higher education—but since 2010 I can no longer make that case.

I have often said about students that you can't teach anyone anything until they are developmentally ready to learn. As applied to myself, I was developmentally ready, finally, at age 55, to consider something I had not before, namely moving on from USC and trying to make some adjustments in my lifestyle, and even work/life balance. I have succeeded in the former, but not so much in the latter. Another line of thinking about career life cycle evolution is better to go when you are at the top of your game than the opposite, an observation that is not original to me. Better to go when people still want you around and before they are anxious for you to leave. Know when to hold and fold 'em.

At the same time, there was the offer from Edgerton of Pew Charitable Trusts to convert my work to a 100% national focus *and* to form a new national organization to pursue this. And, finally, there was a lure of wanting a new challenge and doing this new work with Betsy Barefoot.

These factors, both professional and personal, converged, and I decided to inform the university of my decision to retire. I made an appointment in January of 1999 to see the provost, Jerry Odom, to tell him about my decision to retire and move to North Carolina. I laid out all my reasons, and he was shocked. I understood that. I was shocked too that I was doing this. I was a USC fixture. But I was resolved to proceed. Jerry asked me, "John, what can we do for you?" I told him absolutely nothing more than had already been done for 3 decades. This was not about my salary, or the structure of my position, or seeking another role, or an increased budgetary allocation for my programs. Leader that he was and a quick study of what was being presented to him as a fait accompli, Odom then said, "Well, John, how can we keep you still connected and meaningfully engaged with the university?" Right then and there he offered me an appointment as senior fellow, which I hold to this day, in addition to my faculty appointment as distinguished professor, eventually to be emeritus. The actual duties of the senior fellow appointment were to be determined, but they were to enable my continued counsel to those who would be my successors in leading the University 101 and 401 courses and the research, publishing, and conference organizing of the National Resource Center. I also knew that the university would seek my involvement in other potential "friend-of-the-university" activities such as the ongoing design of the university's Quality Enhancement Program for reaffirmation of accreditation by the Southern Association of Schools and Colleges. And my involvement in this initiative has continued to the present now for more than 2 decades.

The university hosted a retirement party for me, which turned out to be a huge and meaningful event, with about 500 of my USC friends in attendance. It was a truly lovely ceremony, my memories of which I will always cherish. The president, John Palms, told all my friends present these two things:

- I never really knew whom John Gardner worked for; I just knew he worked for the university!
- And I never really knew or understood what John Gardner did; I just knew it was good for our students!

Well, in the big scheme of life and what a 32-year career had amounted to, I guess what he said was what I would have wanted most to be said at this occasion. There was only one exception: I turned to the person sitting next to me, Provost Jerry Odom, and whispered: "Jerry, I know very well whom I work for and it is, thankfully, you!"

What Had My Time and Effort at USC Amounted To?

I believe that my years at USC amounted to the following outcomes, some personal and some professional:

- giving the best years of my life from age 23 to 55 to USC, the only college or university I would ever work for exclusively; this was more time than I would ever be able to give any other employer
- sustaining the original goals and values of a vision for humanizing the university experience through University 101
- providing leadership for the evolution and institutionalizing of University 101—a course that was initially a pet program of one university president, but now is positively correlated with the retention and graduation of thousands of USC students
- disseminating the University 101 concept to hundreds of colleges and universities in the U.S. and around the world
- creating a national center for the improvement of American undergraduate education, the USC National Resource Center for The First-Year Experience and Students in Transition
- founding a national and international conference series
- creating a previously nonexisting scholarly field of research and published scholarship
- developing an educational philosophy and its programmatic outcomes found all over the world: "the first-year experience"
- developing and guiding a special course to support seniors in their transition out of the university, University 401
- expanding what began as a focused initiative to improve student performance in the first year to a focus on multiple student transitions: sophomore, transfer, senior
- continuing the university's quest for social justice in support of the unfinished civil rights movement
- leaving a 198-year-old institution just a little better than I had found it

Isn't this enough? Why did my professional odyssey not stop here? How did this work at USC become the foundation of a new not-for-profit organization? Turn the page for the rest of the story.

For chapter discussion questions, click the link or scan the QR code to visit Appendix C of the Online Compendium.

https://styluspub.presswarehouse.com/uploads/5e35cd13add3605ede5537f
a2a5159aac11d5b57.pdf

20-PLUS YEARS OF NEW WORK—THIS TIME FROM NORTH CAROLINA AND A NEW ORGANIZATION HOME

T his chapter will trace the journey of a great gift, a case of "déjà vu all over again," whereby I, as a higher education student success leader, got a once-in-a-lifetime second opportunity to do it all over again: establish a second higher education organization to advance student success. This was made possible by my leaving my career home, USC; a new marriage to a life partner with whom I could launch such work; and the gifts of multiple philanthropies to invest in our new works. This is about our capstone career experiences through which we will leave a legacy organization to sustain and deepen our work.

Founding a National Organization Redux: The John N. Gardner Institute for Excellence in Undergraduate Education 1999 to the Present

Surely, many readers will have had friends, relatives, and colleagues who have technically "retired" but not really retired from doing remunerative professional work. Given all the changes in the U.S. economy, how and where people can now work, the lengthening of the average life span, coupled with the inadequacy of retirement fixed incomes, what does retirement actually mean? In my case it means continuing to serve higher education on a salaried, full-time basis, with my previous career as an influencing foundation while moving on in many new directions. My nonretirement also has involved working from a new location with a new (but not totally new) life partner. But first I will trace my actual departure from South Carolina.

Moving on From South Carolina

I really had two "senior year experiences": my first as an undergraduate from 1964–1965 and my second, at USC in 1999. Moving on was easier said than done. You don't give 32 years of your life to one cause, in this case higher education in South Carolina, and just throw the switch and move on. In fact, thanks to the senior fellow appointment that Provost Odom awarded me, I haven't totally moved on in the 20-plus years since my technical "retirement" from the state of South Carolina. I am thankful for that structure and continuing invitation to remain involved with USC, which will always be my only university.

My intentional process of "closure" included a series of scheduled, mostly 1-hour "closure conversations" with my closest friends, colleagues, and mentors at the university. They were tremendously helpful to me in terms of integrating and reflecting on what they had meant to me and what we had jointly accomplished.

Starting a New Center: The Policy Center on the First Year of College

Somehow, I had spent 3 decades at a research university and never had much experience with the mother's milk of universities: grants. But I was to get such experience as my mentor, Russ Edgerton, wanted to create a grant for Betsy and me. As I had to learn, foundations don't make grants for individuals; they make them in this case of Pew's policy to other nonprofit-"eligible" organizations. Betsy and I were not a nonprofit, 501c3 organization. This meant that to receive the grant we had to find a 501c3 that would and could accept the grant and then hire us to execute the grant's deliverables. USC was not an option because we would be a married couple working with each other, defined as nepotism and thus prohibited by state's regulations, unless you were a head football coach's son.

We decided to turn then to a 501c3—Brevard College—located in the North Carolina town where we had chosen to live. We met with the president of the college on Easter Sunday in 1999 to broach this possibility. He had never heard of us! Not a good sign. But he was very open to the possibility we offered. This marriage of mutual convenience was to work like this: The foundation would make the grant to the college. The college would then hire us and give us both faculty and administrative appointments. We would pay the college $36,000 a year to rent a duplex apartment to be retrofitted as our office. We would also pay for computing access and support, financial services, and so on. This was definitely a win/win arrangement for a cash-strapped, private college like Brevard, and Betsy and I felt good about helping the college and the community in this manner. The name Edgerton had given this new organization in the first grant he awarded was "The Policy Center on the First Year of College," and we began operations on October 18, 1999.

Not surprisingly, there were no secrets at Brevard College, and we began to sense a reluctance of faculty to embrace our presence. As a "faculty" person, I found this somewhat hard to accept, but I understood. Our small staff of four had a level of "resources" far beyond what all other college employees had access to. For example, we had our own photocopier, just for the four of us. In comparison, the entire college faculty and staff had only one such machine for all of them. And, of course, there was a differential in salaries. We had also been discovered by the college's board of trustees, which wanted us to get engaged in the college's strategic and budgetary planning process, something not appreciated at all by the college's faculty division chairs. We decided then to significantly disengage ourselves but technically remain employees with the college as our fiscal agent.

Our withdrawal from the life of the college was by no means complete. Betsy went on the college's board of trustees, a position she has held for almost 2 decades, and our organization continued to provide a number of pro bono services to the college. In the short run, our presence on the campus did help the institution reputationally, to wit: after 1 year on campus the next annual *U.S. News and World Report* rankings listed Brevard College as number two in the nation for "first-year experience," second only to USC. Hmmm. What a coincidence!

The original grant award was for only 14.5 months with no promise of renewal. The future of the policy center was uncertain, at best. And during that time, our godfather at The Pew Trusts, Edgerton, came to a parting of ways with the foundation's president. Fortunately, before his official resignation, he secured the support of Pew to give us a second grant. I don't know how we would have made it as an organization were it not for that second grant. It takes a long time to launch a nonprofit and to generate the kind of work outcomes that might persuade other philanthropic investors to make awards to your organization.

Another way Edgerton continued to look after us in our earliest years was by "taking" us to another foundation for consideration. This foundation had unique origins in that it had originally been an organization of wealthy individuals organized by a Cornell graduate, Charles "Chuck" Feeney, a billionaire entrepreneur who had the aspiration of giving away all his money during his lifetime. He was best known as the founder of duty-free shops in airports around the world. Feeney's group of like-minded philanthropists was known unofficially as "Anonymous," but they were outed by *The New York Times* in the mid-1990s and became known officially as The Atlantic Philanthropies. Again, Edgerton came to our support by referring us to this foundation, which was located in Ithaca, New York, not coincidentally in proximity to Feeney's alma mater, Cornell. A unique feature of this foundation was that no one could "apply" for a grant from Atlantic. Those desiring a grant had to be "brought to" and "vetted" by the foundation upon some appropriate referral.

Of course, I had prior experience starting a higher education "center," back in 1986–1987. But that was very different experience because I was starting just the most recent of a whole collection of bureaus, centers, and institutes owned by a major research university. USC had all kinds of precedents and policies for the kind of entity that I was going to create. But not little Brevard College. We had to create policies where there were none. For instance, employees at the college traveled so rarely that there was no official travel policy for employees. We had to create one. The college did not have a formal process for what is usually called "contract and grants accounting." We had to establish such a process. We also had to take a building designed to house college students and retrofit it for office functioning.

And that leads me to staffing. We had to hire staff, initially an additional senior leader to complement Betsy and myself, and an administrative support position. And the individual we persuaded to join us for the senior slot was Randy Swing who had higher education knowledge and experience gained over 20 years at Appalachian State University. But he also had a tool belt and vast technical skills; he actually laid the computer cables to make us function. Swing was someone I had come to know from a partnership I developed with Appalachian State circa 1982. I asked the Appalachian State chancellor, Frank Borkowski, who had been my former provost at USC, to give Swing a year's leave to try out working with us. Borkowski supported that idea, and the deal was consummated. Swing had been a senior institutional research officer and involved in Appalachian's first-year seminar. He also had TRIO experience, one more affinity with my work. And he was a risk-taker. Swing was not only very smart; he was also the hardest worker I had ever met other than myself. He was a mainstay with us for 8 years until he left to become the leader for the Association for Institutional Research. One of his goals for us in the Policy Center, at which he was successful, was to teach us "IR speak." Swing helped us look at our higher education work from the perspective of IR by using data, becoming familiar with the IPEDS system, and embedding assessment in all our work.

Laying a Foundation for the Next Level of Organizational Development

As we began our work, we followed a charge we had been given from Edgerton. He urged us to develop the Policy Center so that it would

- not duplicate the work Betsy and I did at USC; complementing that work would be fine, but not duplication
- Create new tools for assessment of the effectiveness of the first year of college
- help institutions take more responsibility for student learning (to offset the historic inclination to hold students 100% responsible for whatever happens for them in college, sometimes known as "blaming the victim")

For the first 3 years, the Policy Center's work focused mainly on the charge to "develop new tools for assessment of the effectiveness first college year." Toward that objective we engaged in several activities. We created, for pro bono use by colleges and universities, a template and process known as "Guidelines for Evaluating the First College Year Experience." We developed cohorts of two- and four-year colleges, public and private in Virginia, North Carolina, Georgia, and Mississippi and a two-year-college cohort in Alabama, to undertake statewide work to use these assessment guidelines to evaluate and improve institutional approaches for the first year and produce recommendations for improvement.

With the University of California, Los Angeles's Higher Education Research Institute (HERI), we developed a new tool for assessment during 2000–2001, still in use today, titled "Your First College Year" (YFCY). This instrument was designed to produce student-level data reporting on students' actual experiences in their first year of college. These data would serve as a posttest to HERI's then 40-year-old highly respected annual "Freshman Survey," which is administered to entering college students to develop baseline data about their plans, goals, and aspirations. We not only compensated HERI for the development of this survey, we also granted them all intellectual property rights to continued survey administration, analyses, and revenue.

With a for-profit company (at the time, Educational Benchmarking, Inc., now Skyfactor, a subsidiary of Macmillan Higher Education), we developed another new tool to measure and then benchmark student perceptions of the first-year seminar. This instrument, known as the First-Year Initiative (FYI) survey, was a tool designed to help both course leaders and instructors benchmark self-reported learning across institutions and courses. During the first year of its use, 41,000 students from 72 institutions participated in the survey generating the first cross-institutional body of evidence about the effectiveness of different elements of the first-year seminar.

In thinking back on our first 3 years as the Policy Center on the First Year of College, I am proud to state that we produced the deliverables for which the center was funded by Pew. We developed assessment tools that are still in use today, we maintained our focus on helping institutions become more responsible for student learning, we became self-sustaining, and we did not duplicate work being done by USC's National Resource Center for The First-Year Experience and Students in Transition.

Creating and Becoming an Independent National Nonprofit Organization

An important evolution of our organization has been our funding model. We were started in 1999 with a total dependency on foundation grants for our support, initially by only one foundation. When we received our first Lumina Foundation grant in 2003 to support our newest initiative, Foundations of Excellence, Lumina program officers were working with us to move the Policy Center toward the goal of being 100% self-sustaining so as not to expect or be dependent on long-term foundation funding. By the time we reached the end of our Lumina grant support in 2008 we had shifted our funding model from 100% grant funded to being 100% funded through an institutional fee-for-services model. This was indeed a notable accomplishment for a relatively small nonprofit organization.

In order to further ensure long-term viability another element of our design had to be our very legal structure itself. The Policy Center's original fiscal host, Brevard College, was indeed hospitable and had done the best to accommodate our presence and needs. However, there were a number of practical shortcomings. One of them became the question of the Policy Center's audited financial structure.

In that regard, in 2007 a new financial auditing firm for the college discovered on the college's books a fairly large cash balance of funds from our grants. I was invited to have an in-person conversation with the college's senior external auditor, Jim Ratchford. The conversation went something like this:

Jim: Hello, my name is Jim Ratchford.

John: And I'm John Gardner.

Jim: And how old are you?

John: 63.

Jim: Do you have a "succession plan?"

John: No!

Jim: Well, you need one. If something were to happen to you, the college (his client) would be vulnerable for having executed contracts for deliverables that, with you out of the picture, the college could not fulfill.

John: Hmmmm.

Jim: Furthermore, there is this matter of who really owns the money. The money is line-itemed under the Policy Center, but technically the college owns the Policy Center and therefore your money. And they are using your money for other purposes (such as maintaining cash flow in the summer to meet payroll by avoiding going into the short-term line-of-credit market). What if the college got a new president who was tempted to take all your money?

John: Well, what alternatives do we have to address this situation?

Jim: Pretty clear and simple: You should consider spinning yourself off and creating your own nonprofit organization!

That's what we did. With the advice of the auditor and a lawyer who specialized in nonprofit organization-related law, we drew up the necessary articles of incorporation, applied to the state of North Carolina to be a registered nonprofit, and secured from the IRS tax-exempt status as a bona fide 501c3 public charity. The Brevard college president, Drew Van Horn, was most accommodating and agreed that this was the best path forward for both the college and our small organization. Neither he nor I wanted there to be any ambiguity about who was responsible for the grants we received and whose money this really was. In order to consummate this transition we had to go through a process very similar to a marital divorce that would include a property settlement, disposition and transfer of assets, and so forth. Having been twice divorced and remarried myself, I was no stranger to this process. The parallels were quite striking.

Of course, a very important step in this evolution was to create our own governing board. That board today has 13 "external" members who serve for fixed terms, and three "internal," two of whom are life-term members—Betsy Barefoot and I. Our board, by law, must have an annual meeting, but we meet more frequently, usually three to four phone or video meetings and one in-person meeting per year.

What Is in an Organizational Name? Everything

Another major decision was determining a legal name for this new nonprofit organization. Betsy and I sought the counsel of a number of good thinkers, and we were advised to consider naming the organization for me. This was a challenge for whatever degree of modesty that I had. But I became persuaded by others that my name had value as a kind of brand and that the higher education community was well familiar with my work and reputation, especially in terms of my educational values. It was easily understood and assumed that I, and especially an organization named for me, would be tireless advocates and champions for all undergraduate students, but especially those who were instead less fortunate and less advantaged. The kind of work we would offer and its quality and impact would also be well understood, especially the focus of that work on social justice outcomes for "students in transition" in the first-year, sophomore, transfer, and senior year experiences. Hence the name we decided to give our new organization was the John N. Gardner Institute for Excellence in Undergraduate Education. The plan was that the name, mission, and work would carry on beyond the point when I ceased leading the organization.

At the time of this writing, we are contemplating a foray into a new initiative that would take us beyond a strict "undergraduate" focus, namely the issue of graduate student retention and graduation outcomes, particularly for underserved populations. Assuming that plan moves forward we may need to revise our organizational name and simply be designated as an Institute for Excellence in *Higher* Education. Time and circumstances will tell. Regardless of the ultimate breadth of our foci, the original design was to create an organizational and brand identity that could be sustainable beyond my literal leadership for the organization. It was the hope when we started our current organization that its work would transcend my leadership and life, but always be associated with the educational values for which I had stood. And that is still the plan.

Running a Nonprofit Organization Like a Business

One of the biggest changes for me as a higher education administrative leader has been to remember that I no longer get to live financially on an annual appropriation from the legislature and some kind of budgetary allocation from my host university. For the past 23 years I have been ultimately responsible for generating the resources for everything we need. I no longer had a huge professional-expert ecosystem to call on as a privilege of being part of a university. If the institute needs a lawyer, auditor, facilities design expert, additional office space, or technology consultation, I/we have to assume the costs for all of these operational requisites. I and institute staff have to earn every cent of our support.

In addition, we must take ultra-seriously our tax-exempt mission as a public charity. This means that our primary organizational mission is *not* to make money, and we *must* and do provide some services pro bono on a noncost-recovery basis. For example, we provide to national audiences at no charge a series of virtual "transformative conversations" and a series on improving transfer. We also produce a series of podcasts called "Office Hours With John Gardner" featuring conversations with educational innovators. In addition, we sponsor annual award processes to identify both individual and institutional innovators whose work we share in a complimentary video format. We have offered gratis webinars on what we are calling "Stories of Hope," focusing on California social justice efforts in higher education; and for the higher education community in Ohio a virtual seminar and publication to drive actions on the topic of "the role of faculty in student success." Finally, we are offering, a year-long professional development process for chief academic officers of colleges and universities to help them transform into both vice presidents for academic affairs *and* innovation.

Even though we do not receive state funding, members of the public are still our shareholders. Yes, we do need money. But that is not the end; it is a means. One of our former board members regularly reminded me that "not-for-profit is a legal tax status but it should not be an operational mind-set." I get the message; we must be "business like" even though we are not a for-profit business. Instead, legally and culturally, we are emphatically and proudly, a not-for-profit corporation.

Operationally, for me this means the following:

- We have to provide services that the market needs and will support. It is possible for us, through our innovative and entrepreneurial thinking, to both generate the needs in the marketplace for our new services and then fulfill those needs.

- We must live within our means. At the same time, we are as generous as possible with whatever revenue successes we achieve in terms of our staff compensation and benefits.
- We do not incur debt.
- We invest only in investment vehicles that return a guaranteed fixed income.
- We put our money in our people and not fancy "digs." Unlike state agencies, we don't put significant resources in furniture in lieu of compensation.
- All of us spend our organizational money as if it is our own. Because it is.
- We are proud of our annual audit. Our goal is to have the highest levels of financial integrity as possible with no substantive findings regarding any deficiencies with respect to the established generally accepted accounting principles of effective financial management. In other words, I/we aspire to and consistently achieve an annual "clean audit."
- We are as transparent as possible with all members of our staff about our financial resources, how we are doing, and what our annual financial goals and needs are.
- We don't spend everything we have. An annual operating surplus is always a goal, coupled with adequate reserves that could keep us afloat in hard times. By way of illustration, we had no layoffs, terminations, or reductions in compensation in either the Great Recession of 2008 or the COVID-19 pandemic period in 2020–2022.

For most faculty who have led traditional academic lives, this kind of shift in mindset might have been difficult. But for me, thank goodness, it came very naturally because at USC I did administer multiple continuing education operations that were not funded by state dollars and hence had to be self-supporting. I had learned that we had to have conferences and publications that higher education consumers were willing to buy. In other words, I had already learned a great deal about how to be, in the contemporary parlance, "self-sustaining."

Advancing Our Work With Support From Foundations and Institutions

Support from foundations meant that when I accepted a gift from a philanthropy I was legally, professionally, and reputationally agreeing to produce what are known in the grants world as "deliverables." I love this concept even though it doesn't really translate to the traditional academic world. Most of us in the professoriate do not think of ourselves being obligated to produce "deliverables." But for me this has been a powerful motivator of which I am mindful every day!

I have also learned that foundations are like colleges and universities in that they have boards of directors and senior executives, including those to whom I "report," known as "program officers." Like colleges and universities these foundation personnel manifest changing priorities. Therefore, a foundation that just awarded you a grant might well have a change in strategic grant-making priorities and philosophy in the middle of your work for them. This means that just because you were fortunate enough to receive one grant doesn't automatically entitle you to a second. We are not too big to fail. We do not have tenure with any funder. That too was an adjustment for me. I was used to having tenure, a form of life-long support for me from my employer.

Another dynamic of note is that early program officers had to explain to me that technically I didn't work for them. They don't give the grant to individuals, because that's not what the law allows. Instead, the legal basis of the grant is that it is given to another organization, which, in turn may employ me. I must confess, I have never really bought into these correct legal technicalities. I view the program officers as being people I work for, even though technically I don't. I feel obligated and loyal to them. I owe them something! And I am going to produce that deliverable.

I have also learned that program officers have bosses too. These officers have to show results to their executives and especially boards for return on investments. Thus, there are risks in making investments in organizations when you don't know or have any history with the people involved. What this means practically is you are more likely to be funded if your work is known, if you are trusted to do what you say you are going to do, and if you have documented expertise and a track record. I found this means that it really takes quite a while to develop a reputation within the relatively small world of program officers who work for foundations that invest in higher education, especially in the student success subculture of higher education.

I also learned early in my work leading a nonprofit that some foundations may discourage a long-term dependency on them for funding. Hence, in the early years of our development we understood that a major goal, as stated by our program officers, was that we would become self-sustaining and able to support ourselves not solely by grants but also through a fee-for-services model. The grants we received from The Pew Charitable Trusts, The Atlantic Philanthropies, Lumina Foundation for Education, Winthrop Rockefeller Foundation, and USA Funds from 1999 to 2008 came with the assumption that by the completion of the grant we would have become operationally independent from grant funding. We did achieve that goal, and in spite of the arrival of the Great Recession in 2008, that was our funding model from 2008 through 2016.

By 2016, as an organization we had evolved significantly and had a great deal to show prospective investors in terms of numbers and types of services we were successfully providing the academy. By then we had been in business for 17 years, and I had personally accumulated about 50 years of experience. We also had other staff members who had developed reputations attractive to funders, especially my spouse, Betsy Barefoot, and our newer colleague, Drew Koch. It would be accurate to say that by 2016 we had been "discovered." That ushered in the period 2016–2022 during which we again became primarily, but by no means totally, funded by grants. During this period, we have enjoyed the support of Ascendium Foundation, the Bill and Melinda Gates Foundation, ECMC Foundation, Kresge Foundation, Lumina Foundation for Education, and the Schusterman Family Foundation. Our business model has been further complemented by a number of very important contracts for services to major higher education systems, most notably the University System of Georgia and the Kentucky Community Technical College System. And this is in addition to even more revenue from fees paid by the almost 500 institutions we have served.

What Exactly Is Our Business at the Gardner Institute?

Betsy Barefoot and I have provided a number of "exhibitor" sessions at the annual Conference on the First-Year Experience. These are essentially commercial pitches for the services provided by the institute. While I love the practice of public speaking and am proud of what we have accomplished, I have tirelessly labored to have us not be seen as "vendors" and "selling" in the classic sense. But in reality, we are competing in this market space in which the vast majority of our competitors are for-profit companies. Literally then, we are "selling"—especially ideas. I realize that is what I have always been "selling," in the sense of persuading and exhorting fellow educators to adopt an educational values position and take specific actions. This is what I argue the Gardner Institute is selling:

- big ideas
- experience
- knowledge—experience and research-based publishing
- academic credibility
- campus leadership and teaching experience
- relationships

- strategies
- wisdom
- inspiration
- an organizational emphasis on academic success
- an equity and social justice focus

It All Comes Down to Organizational Mission: Advancing Social Justice

I am driven every day by the mission of my employing organization. This board-approved mission is as follows:

> The John N. Gardner Institute for Excellence in Undergraduate Education is a non-profit organization dedicated to partnering with colleges, universities, philanthropic organizations, educators, and other entities to increase institutional responsibility for improving outcomes associated with teaching, learning, retention, and completion. Through its efforts, the Institute will strive to advance higher education's larger goal of increasing student academic success and thereby achieving equity and social justice.

Finally, I have a job where I have bosses (the institute's governing board) who won't fire me because of my commitment to advancing social justice! Looking back, I achieved a high level of professional security in 1977 when I was awarded tenure by USC. And time and time again, I witnessed my USC leaders taking strong public stands to the board and the general public in support of academic freedom and in support of my own professional conduct when it came to matters dealing with the Athletic Department and the sexual health decision-making topics of the University 101 course.

But the level of support I have received as an autonomous, nonprofit, higher education chief executive officer from my governing board has been truly extraordinary. Actually, this has not only been "support" but also making such action an official expectation that I lead an organization in pursuit of greater social justice and equity. They have my back. I truly could not ask for anything more in this regard. My board has not only directed its expectations toward me, the board members have provided valuable and seasoned counsel about how we can attain this mission. And it is truly empowering.

These expectations permeate the whole organization. We are all very mission driven. We frequently quote parts of the mission and explicitly describe to ourselves and our external partners how what we are thinking, saying, writing, and doing is mission consistent. The period of having a racist, xenophobic, U.S. president clearly influenced our public-facing language and positions. But the level of our intense specificity about living our mission was also given a huge push forward by these events in 2020–2021:

- the terrible scourge of the COVID-19 pandemic and how it revealed like nothing before the vast inequities in all areas of American society
- the murders of Black Americans in 2020 by White law enforcement officials and other citizens
- the Black Lives Matter movement and the overwhelming degree of support that it received from the U.S. public
- the blatantly racist tone and substance of the U.S. presidential election campaign
- the storming of the U.S. Capitol on January 6, 2021
- the subsequent efforts after the inauguration of the new president to adopt new policies at the state levels to suppress voting rights and access, about which we have a public-facing statement on the institute website expressing opposition
- the increasing public support for undertaking significant philosophical and policy changes regarding a vast array of social issues, including higher education
- the participation of the Gardner Institute in the Bill and Melinda Gates Intermediaries for Scale initiative, which has helped our organizational self-study, assessment, and planning to be much more intentional about our equity mission

I can only conclude that here in the capstone period of my career the stars have aligned and there has never been a better time in my country for me to work even harder to do what I can in my continuing locus of control to advance social justice through leadership of an organization dedicated to that proposition. It occurs to me that in the sense of a constant awareness of being mission-focused every single day of my work, I have returned to my 20s when I was in the U.S. Air Force. I am still aware every day of my organizational mission to do work that is of redeeming social value. Life can come full circle.

Returning to an International Focus: The Global Forum for Student Success

From 1977 to 1990 at USC I was greatly influenced by an institution-wide emphasis on global engagement spearheaded by the university president. During that period, as I have described earlier, I established a series of international conferences on the first-year experience. USC and University 101 also attracted higher education professionals from other parts of the world to spend a sabbatical term at the university, learning from us and us from them. In that vein we hosted a number of visitors anxious to learn about our success with the first-year experience. Although as a free-standing organization the Gardner Institute is overwhelmingly focused on U.S. activities, we have hosted visitors from overseas, and we have also provided Gardner Institute advisory services to institutions in Canada and Mexico and in places as far away as Qatar and the Marshall Islands. While we are predominantly focused on serving U.S. institutions, we have the interest, ability, and willingness to be engaged beyond the United States.

I will confess that since leaving the work I founded at USC, the only substantive change my successors made that I regret was the decision in 2011 to get out of the international conferencing business. I ruminated over this for some time, and finally in 2020, partly in reaction to the official U.S. government policy of "America First" and institutionalized xenophobia, I resolved to get the Gardner Institute engaged internationally.

Like almost everything else we do, I decided to call on a potential partner, in this case, Elon University's director of its Center for Engaged Learning and professor of history, Peter Felten. Felten is a highly competent, sought-after faculty development and thought leader in undergraduate education. Felten had already been very influential on a number of the components of the Gardner Institute's Teaching and Learning Academy, and Betsy Barefoot and I also had the pleasure of working with Felten, Leo Lambert, and Charles Schroeder, on a 2016 book concerning "what matters most" in undergraduate education.

What Felten and I have done, for which the jury, as of this writing, is still out, is to launch and establish what we are calling a "Global Forum on Student Success." Our founders are an eclectic group of about two dozen educators from Australia, Canada, Colombia, Ireland, Portugal, Singapore, South Africa, the United Kingdom (England and Scotland), and the United States. We are refining our mission, definition of problems on which we will focus, and means for including student voices and are delineating a number of action focus projects. Our goals are to serve both individual members' institutional interests and their respective nations' higher education systems, all in the name of advancing both access and success in tertiary education and the global cause of social justice. This is another wonderful capstone activity for me.

Consulting: An Additional Delivery Mode for My Mission

I have come to see myself as an incognito higher education detective. I look for the clues to the institutional culture, and they are very easy to spot. One of my standard practices is to prepare for class. That means doing "home-work" on the institution before setting my feet on the campus, so that I can honestly claim to an audience that I know more about the facts of the place than 50% of the people in the audience. This is relatively easy to do. It just takes time and knowing what to ask for—what a recovering former history teacher like me would call "the primary sources." Every institution and every-one in the place have a story. The best consultants have to get the story right. You also have to have a story yourself and tell it as is appropriate.

Where does my expertise come from? From years and years of experi-ence. My 40-plus years of consulting work have taken me to over 500 institu-tions in the United States, Canada, Denmark, Ireland, Norway, Qatar, and the United Kingdom. I realized after making a number of consulting visits that it was kind of like being back in the Air Force psychiatric clinic again. Once I had had some experience there and seen multiple patients of the same diagnostic category, I could identify human types much more rapidly, while still allowing for human individual differences and uniqueness. It's the same with institutions: Once I had visited enough of them, I could see that they fell into categories by the nature of the problems they were experiencing in achieving—or not achieving—acceptable levels of student success. Most importantly, as with my military patients, the consultant has to have seen the right kind of interventions and strategies for improvement. I realize that this analogy between the needs of college and university campuses with the mental health needs of active-duty military personnel and dependents may not appear flattering to higher education, but I assure you that there are many valid parallels.

For me, consulting has been a never-ending source of new learning and personal development. And this kind of knowledge and service is part of what I am providing through the nonprofit organization that Betsy and I founded. This is tremendously gratifying work, and I have formed a large number of very special relationships with clients. We share in common the kinds of outcomes we want to achieve for our students. The former clients, now colleagues and friends, share with me high levels of institutional loyalty and many other affinities. I know this is a not a modest self-description, but hey, we are all really good at something!

The Long Journey to a Succession Plan

Another key step in the continuing evolution and sustainability of our own, independent nonprofit organization status with long-term shelf life was to go back and address the question first posed to me by our new auditor in 2007: "Do you have a succession plan?" The answer at that time was no, but

privately to myself I said, "I am working on it." This was an extremely important consideration for me and Betsy, as it is and should be to any founders of
a successful and innovative new start-up organization. Finally, in 2010, we
decided to advance a succession plan for the next generation of our institute
beyond Betsy's and my founding period.

While of course Betsy and I and our board of directors had the option
to do a national search to perhaps find an unknown leader, this was not
something we wanted to gamble on. Therefore, we decided to cast about
for someone we knew well and proactively recruit such transitional leadership. We had a number of criteria in mind. We needed a successor who was
younger than me in order to give the institute long-term stability. Yes, I know
age is not supposed to be a factor, but that was a key reality of why we were
engaging in this process in the first place. We needed a successor who knew
the student success field—both in terms of practice and scholarship—a
successor with integrity who would share my values and my commitment to
social justice based in a strong liberal arts education. Experience in writing,
communicating, and managing grants was essential. And finally, we sought
someone who was personable and could create and maintain relationships
with our staff and partnerships with external organizations.

We reached out to a married couple, to be the next husband/wife leadership team for our organization, Drew and Sara Stein Koch, of Purdue
University. Drew (who is 25 years younger than I) was to be my heir apparent. Sara would work less than full-time as long as they had children still at
home. And children they did have, six of them, three adopted from China
and Latvia. Both of them had held responsible administrative posts at Purdue
and met all the criteria. Betsy and I had worked closely with Drew in the
early 90s when he was one of our master's-level graduate students at USC.
We saw very clearly what he was intellectually capable of and had stayed in
touch with him after his time at USC. This couple was a great hire, and they
remain the future of the institute's leadership. Thus, about 10 years after they
joined us, I requested our board of directors in September of 2021 to name
Drew to be my official successor as the chief executive officer, and I have been
reconstituted to the full-time role of executive chair and founder.

My self-description of "the jury is in" is one I use frequently to describe
where I am in both my career and life as of this writing. I do not mean that
I have finally "arrived" and can now be complacent and stop having goals
and interests in new forms of mission-consistent work. I have never at any
point in my professional life had a specific set of goals that would suggest
a conventional career ladder in terms of upwardly mobile leadership roles.
In that respect, I am very happy where I am right now. I want to remain
doing the few things that I am really good at for as long as I can. I have a

unique leadership role in American higher education, and I have no desire to do anything else, anywhere else, even if another organization would have me. All my major life decisions have been made and the jury is in on all of them. I have, as the saying goes, "wintered into wisdom." Nevertheless, I wonder, what more I can still accomplish and contribute in my career? How will I adjust if and when I ever retire? What will I do with all my brag-wall memorabilia? One thing I know for sure is that I have many actions I wish to continue to take in pursuit of my personal and our organizational mission.

Increasing Student Success Will Take All of Us

Here, in the capstone period of my career, I am having the thrill of seeing the focus of my lifetime work, student success, especially focused on equity in attainment, finally receiving much more institutional, national, and international attention. With this, though, comes understandably an increase in resentment by others for what I on some level represent, namely the fact that I am White, and male, aging, privileged by my positions, and affluent by virtue of my upbringing. I will be the first to admit that White men in America created the inequitable state of affairs that we are now trying to rectify. And I will acknowledge the validity of the argument many make that we White men can never have the desirable level of empathy, knowledge, and understanding of what it means to be poor, disadvantaged, and discriminated against as those who were born into far less advantaged positions. Guilty as charged!

But I would counter that people like me have the capacity to transcend our origins and develop the necessary capacities, as I have been able to do, to make positive contributions to the advancement of all students, including and especially our least advantaged students. And because of the power, influence, and leverage we have retained, we still have considerable power to advance the student success movement for sustainability, mainstreaming, and greater levels of impact.

I have written this book in the spirit of inviting other postsecondary educators to join this student success effort, no matter at what stage of their careers they might find themselves or what their backgrounds might have been. And I have had a special message for those citizens who are most like I was in childhood: White and affluent, with no expectation or encouragement to ever enter a profession in pursuit of social justice. I have never been poor or disadvantaged or personally discriminated against. But I have been effective at this work nevertheless and believe that others like me not only can but must get aboard. I hope my many illustrations and suggestions in this book will encourage many educators—from all backgrounds—to join this cause.

You are needed. Our students deserve you, and not as many will advance without you.

For chapter discussion questions, click the link or scan the QR code to visit Appendix C of the Online Compendium.

https://styluspub.presswarehouse.com/uploads/5e35cd13add3605ede5537f
a2a5159aac11d5b57.pdf

CONCLUSION

I never intended this book to be just about me. It was my greatest hope that these reflections on my part, coupled with implicit and sometimes explicit advice, would help other aspiring and current college and university educators who want to be contributors to the still emerging field of student success. We can't have too many good examples or too much inspiration for producing more educators who will be passionate about this work.

It matters not where you are in your career: precareer, early, mid, advanced/senior. I am seeing educators at all stages of their careers joining the integrated equity/student success movement. And this is being driven by an institutional market need and thus demand, and by individual educator motivation and inspiration to want to contribute to the redesign of higher education for achievement of greater equity. This is also being driven, thankfully, by the change in national climate as a consequence of the tumult of 2020 and resulting changes in U.S. political leadership. One of the things that I know without a doubt is there will be more students needing the kind of support, advocacy, and commitment that competent student success practitioners and leaders like those of you reading this book can and will provide.

Of course, each of us is unique, and none of us have paths into and through our careers that are exactly alike. But many of us have had certain preparation routes for entry into the student success field and experiences that have been successful and replicable. What then have I learned from my own career path that I think could be used by others and is definitely not unique to me?

Here are a number of suggestions for your consideration. I am not saying that I think one should have to do all of these things! I am not asking anyone to be me. My career allowed me to be me. I would want your career to allow you to be you so that you feel congruency between your choice of values, hopes, dreams, and aspirations; your life's work to date; and those with whom you will be working and serving.

Develop a personal philosophy of education. Be clear about what you believe, revise your beliefs as necessary throughout your career, and share your philosophy with your students and those who report to you. Ideally, you should reduce

175

this to writing and share at appropriate times with appropriate audiences. I include my own such statement in the online compendium to this book.

Develop the requisite knowledge, experience, and skills base. You have to know something at least, and preferably a great deal, about what it takes to produce successful college students. Yes, you can study this as a field of knowledge. What do such students do in college? And what do institutions do that produce successful graduates, especially those whose entering characteristics would suggest a lower probability of success? What are the strategies, experiences, bodies of knowledge, and skills that we need to provide our students to help them be successful in college? How do you secure this kind of knowledge? There are many routes to this objective, but perhaps your education is the most important route.

Get as much formal higher education as possible. It will be more difficult for you to advance if you do not obtain a terminal degree or whatever others might judge to be the equivalent in accomplishments. I realize this suggestion sounds pretty obvious. It is. If you are a master's student in higher education or student personnel services, consider doing your terminal degree in a discipline that would enable you to ultimately seek a tenure-track faculty position. I offer this suggestion because I see the realignment of some student support functions from student affairs to student success and the leadership of these new units being exercised by individuals with faculty rank. We are working in a subculture that exalts the most advanced levels of certified knowledge and still awards highest status, and thus influence on students, to those with faculty rank.

Try to get an early or precareer experience in a highly effective mission-driven organization. This would immerse you in a work setting with people of all walks of life and social strata, and in which you will learn that the overall good of the group and its mission takes precedence over your individual needs and aspirations. The U.S. military is the best example that I can think of for doing this.

Work in some capacity with students who are less likely to otherwise be successful in college. This means you need to have taught, advised, counseled, supervised, programmed activities for, lived with, recruited these students. In my experience the single most valuable experience I had may have been my actually living in residence one summer with high school–age Upward Bound students. I learned more in just one summer about what it means to be a poor, Black kid growing up in a southern town than from anything else I had done or could have done. I especially learned the meaning and power of the concept of "community" in a subculture that has been historically discriminated against and has lived in fear, especially from the police and more broadly from "authority."

Gain teaching experience with high-risk students. This means you have to have the credentials and aptitude for some experience as a faculty member. I have found that academics with some teaching history, coupled with other types of experience in student success work, are advancing furthest and fastest.

Try, if applicable, to gain tenure. Personally, I found that to be a tenured faculty member of the highest professorial rank gave me access and opportunity to influence the most important institutional decisions for advancing student success. This status also gave me the professional and personal freedom to challenge the status quo that often does not promote equity for students most in need. My nontenured colleagues could never have taken the kinds of risks I took without some negative career repercussions.

Take your earned sabbatical. If you are a tenured faculty member eligible for a sabbatical, by all means take one and spend a term or a year in an exciting place doing student success work. I didn't do this and I should have.

Read everything you can in what is now the extensive student success literature. This includes books and articles that claim to be reporting on "best practices" and "high-impact practices." To the extent you can, try to make contributions to that literature.

Volunteer to be a reviewer for journals in fields connected to student success. This will enable you to help other educators further their intellectual preparation for this work. It will also give you ideas about what topics need further development and research.

Attend conferences where there is a focus on student success and equity initiatives. There are plenty of choices, more all the time. The "student success" theme is showing up as a session track, even in organizational gatherings for which this consideration is not a primary emphasis. Submit a proposal to present your own work at such a meeting and learn from the feedback you will surely receive.

Visit other institutions that are similar to, or different from, yours. See what you can learn from their student success work.

Volunteer to your accreditor for training as a member of a visiting accreditation team. Accreditors are constantly calling for volunteers to serve in this important role.

Develop skills in conducting assessment. Assessment experience is more important than ever as a prerequisite for career advancement.

Engage in research on student success. This could be at your own institution or elsewhere. If you are in a doctoral program, consider such topics for your dissertation.

Apply assessment findings to the decisions you make for improvement of initiatives you oversee. Above all, if you conducted the assessment tell others what you did, why, and what you learned. Show them you take assessment seriously as a way of practicing improvement, including both your successes and failures.

Report your findings in writing, preferably through academic publishing. Publishing is still the currency of the realm.

Find others doing cutting-edge program development, research, and/or publishing. See if you can join the effort in any capacity. The worst that can happen is if they say no thank you.

Seek opportunities to travel, study, attend conferences abroad. Seeing how other cultures attempt to improve student success will help you escape your own natural ethnocentrism. Take every opportunity to visit higher education settings outside the United States. This can help you rethink how you see our higher education realities and to consider them in a much less U.S.-centric frame of reference

Mystery-shop other institutions. When driving in some new region and noticing a road sign for a college you've never visited, get off the road, take a self-guided tour, find some students, and talk to them. Visit the admissions office and pretend that you are looking for a college on behalf of a relative.

Take the opportunity to participate in professional development programs. Ideally connect with those offered by your teaching/learning faculty/staff development center. Most of us were not taught either to understand or teach today's students, and we need all the help we can get. Great teachers, staff, and leaders are made, not born. If you are a faculty member and your institution offers graduate work in the study of higher education, college student personnel services, take a course in student development theory. It will open you up to new ways of thinking about serving students.

Become involved in institution-wide projects. These will get you out of your silo and involve you in processes that integrate faculty, academic/student success/student affairs administrators, and staff. You will observe and learn a great deal that will advance you in student success work. And you will discover wonderful new colleagues and friends you wouldn't have otherwise. You will be good for them, and they for you.

Be constantly on the lookout for "roller bag moments." My moment was noting that there was not a conference I could attend for educators who wanted to focus on improving first-year college student success, and hence I organized one myself that became the platform for a higher education reform movement. Just as I found my moment for inspiration, so can you.

Establish an advisory stakeholder group for any initiative or unit for which you are responsible. Student success leaders are usually only as good as the advice they get from dedicated colleagues supporting your work by lending their imprimatur, advice, and feedback.

Engage in partnerships with other people, units, and organizations. Lone rangers rarely make it to the top in student success work. Collaboration will yield far richer dividends in the long run than competition.

No matter how far you advance, never get so far up that you lose regular contact with students. If you fail to maintain contact with them, you might as well be working for a bank or an insurance company. If you have a faculty appointment and become a student success administrator, do not totally give up all your teaching duties. I always taught at least one class a term.

Find opportunities to both observe students and listen to them. To the extent possible, occasionally mystery shop your own institution to find out what students are really experiencing. Find contexts and ways to spend time with students, especially in spontaneous and informal contexts.

Solicit informal feedback. Seek this from students, faculty, and staff, especially those who come from different socioeconomic, racial, ethnic, and cultural backgrounds from yours. Find out how you are coming across to them and act on their feedback. You need to know just how they see you.

Improve your understanding of why some students don't succeed. If you were like many higher educators who initially thrived in college, you must take compensatory steps to understand why and how many college students flounder and are not as successful as you were.

Strive to improve your understanding of students who are less privileged than you are and/or were. Such understanding, ideally, can become the basis for authentic empathy, which is empowering for yourself and others.

Find a student success equity mentor. Find someone in the student success world you really respect and see if they will take you on as a mentee. There has been no time in my career that I haven't needed mentors, including the present. Yes, and I still have one with whom I interact and am inspired by regularly. Don't be reluctant to ask. Many leaders like to be sought out in this manner and find gratification in serving in this capacity. The worst that could happen could be the individual you ask declines but recommends a substitute who could turn out to be an even better fit for you. I actually regard mentorship as one of my most important duties to others and to the academy which I serve. It is the most personal and powerful teaching I have experienced, both on the giving and receiving end.

Be a mentor to others. Just as you have hopefully been fortunate enough to have found special people to show interest in you and adopt you as a mentee, return the gift when you have appropriate opportunities to do so in your career. You will learn, grow, and be inspired by what you learn from your mentees, just as you were by your mentors. We all want to bring others forward. And if we are ever to achieve anything like equity in the academy, more of us are going to have to open the doors to equity for others through mentoring. There is much evidence that people who are officially and formally mentored advance faster and further. An important concomitant to mentoring is to use your formal power to offer people new positions in which they can grow, perhaps reporting to you. A variation on this theme is to be really conscientious about offering to nominate others for position vacancies and/or writing letters of reference. After 56 years there is not a week that goes by that I don't write a letter for someone. And I should; people once wrote for me! This is one of my most truly important duties of academic collegiality.

What does this all come down to? I think it is that we must act on the recognition that yes, students do have to ultimately take responsibility for their own learning. But they are not responsible alone. What matters equally is the responsibility we educators and our institutions take for the achievement of student success. This means you. Each of us has to do everything we can in our own locus of control, spheres of influence, at any and all points in our career to take concrete actions to increase student success. And all of us are needed by students to help advance social justice, those of us from both advantaged and less advantaged backgrounds. As we all go forward together, so goes the substance and future of our democracy and its higher education system.

For chapter discussion questions, click the link or scan the QR code to visit Appendix C of the Online Compendium.

https://styluspub.presswarehouse.com/uploads/5e35cd13add3605ede5537f
a2a5159aac11d5b57.pdf

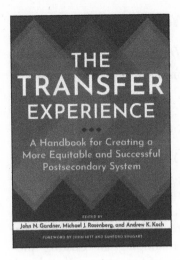

The Transfer Experience

A Handbook for Creating a More Equitable and Successful Postsecondary System

Edited by John N. Gardner, Michael J. Rosenberg, and Andrew K. Koch

Foreword by John Hitt and Sanford Shugart

Copublished With Gardner Institute

"*The Transfer Experience* is a gift to educators who view transfer as a social justice imperative. Transfer matters now, perhaps more than ever, and the text offers the most comprehensive, evidence-based analysis of the transfer experience. The authors offer a transformational view of the transfer journey that goes beyond a mechanistic, processual experience. Shattering outmoded transfer assumptions, the authors take care to present a more thoughtful, holistic view of transfer keeping in mind that underserved, first-generation, adult learners should be assisted in every way to fulfill their hopes and dreams of earning a bachelor's degree. The text offers fertile ground for significant equity and justice dialogue, transformational changes, and policy considerations."—***Laura I. Rendón**, Author of* Sentipensante Pedagogy: Educating for Wholeness, Social Justice and Liberation, *Stylus*

"This book is a timely and much-needed call to action to more effectively meet the transfer needs of our postsecondary students. The research contained within these chapters presents a playbook for both campus and state higher education officials to create and execute a strategy that will better serve students, campuses and states alike."—***Robert E. Anderson**, President, SHEEO, State Higher Education Executive Officers Association*

The First-Year Seminar

Designing, Implementing, and Assessing Courses to Support Student Learning and Success

5-Volume Set

The First-Year Seminar: Designing, Implementing, and Assessing Courses to Support Student Learning and Success, a five-volume series, is designed to assist educators who are interested in launching a first-year seminar or revamping an existing program. Each volume examines a different aspect of first-year seminar design or administration and offers suggestions for practice grounded in research on the seminar, the literature on teaching and learning, and campus-based examples. Because national survey research suggests that the seminar exists in a variety of forms on college campuses—and that some campuses combine one or more of these forms to create a hybrid seminar—the series offers a framework for decision making rather than a blueprint for course design.

The set includes:
Volume I: *Designing and Administering the Course*
Volume II: *Instructor Training and Development*
Volume III: *Teaching in the First-Year Seminar*
Volume IV: *Using Peers in the Classroom*
Volume V: *Assessing the First-Year Seminar*

The University 101 Faculty Resource Manual, 2022

Edited by Daniel B. Friedman and Kristy Sokol

A publication of University 101 Programs, University of South Carolina

The University 101 Faculty Resource Manual, 2022 is the 13th edition of the publication and builds off previous versions. This edition has been updated to reflect best practices for teaching a first-year seminar. The first nine chapters constitute the "textbook" for U101 instructors and were written by University 101 Programs Staff.

Each of the 10 learning outcome chapters were developed by committees with diverse representation from across campus based on their expertise, review of literature and best practices, and approaches that have worked well in past years. The manual is updated each year based on assessment data indicating which approaches work best for achieving course outcomes.

To order the PDF, please send an email request to stylusinfo@styluspub .com that includes your full name, billing address, and phone number. We will call you to obtain your payment information, after which we will email you the PDF.

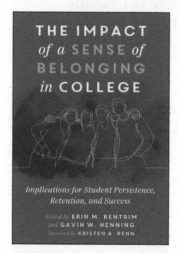

The Impact of a Sense of Belonging in College

Implications for Student Persistence, Retention, and Success

Edited by Erin M. Bentrim and Gavin W. Henning

Foreword by Kristen A. Renn

Sense of belonging refers to the extent a student feels included, accepted, valued, and supported on their campus. The developmental process of belonging is interwoven with the social identity development of diverse college students. Moreover, belonging is influenced by the campus environment, relationships, and involvement opportunities as well as a need to master the student role and achieve academic success.

Although the construct of sense of belonging is complex and multilayered, a consistent theme across the chapters in this book is that the relationship between sense of belonging and intersectionality of identity cannot be ignored, and must be integrated into any approach to fostering belonging.

Over the past 10 years, colleges and universities have started grappling with the notion that their approaches to maintaining and increasing student retention, persistence, and graduation rates were no longer working. As focus shifted to uncovering barriers to student success while concurrently recognizing student success as more than solely academic factors, the term "student sense of belonging" gained traction in both academic and cocurricular settings. The editors noticed the lack of a consistent definition, or an overarching theoretical approach, as well as a struggle to connect disparate research. A compendium of research, applications, and approaches to sense of belonging did not exist, so they brought this book into being to serve as a single point of reference in an emerging and promising field of study.

22883 Quicksilver Drive
Sterling, VA 20166-2019   Subscribe to our email alerts: www.Styluspub.com